GW01161474

DOVER LIBRARY
TEL 204241

11/97

04. JUN 93

03. JUL 98

31. DEC 98

28. JAN 99

02. DEC

Deleted

(50p)

DOVER LIBRARY
TEL 204241

KENT
COUNTY
LIBRARY

306. 874

COLLINS, S.

Step-parents

and their children

Books should be returned or renewed by the last
date stamped above.

C 15 0543714

STEP-PARENTS AND THEIR CHILDREN

HUMAN HORIZONS SERIES

STEP-PARENTS
AND
THEIR CHILDREN

Stephen Collins

A CONDOR BOOK
SOUVENIR PRESS (E & A) LTD

Copyright © 1988 by Stephen Collins

First published 1988 by Souvenir Press
(Educational & Academic) Ltd,
43 Great Russell Street, London WC1B 3PA
and simultaneously in Canada

All Rights Reserved. No part of this publication
may be reproduced, stored in a retrieval system,
or transmitted, in any form or by any means, electronic,
mechanical, photocopying, recording or otherwise without
the prior permission of the Copyright owner

ISBN 0 285 65057 2 hardback
ISBN 0 285 65058 0 paperback

Photoset and printed in Great Britain by
WBC Print Ltd, Bristol

'Hearts are not had as a gift, but hearts are earned . . .'
W.B. Yeats, *Prayer for my Daughter*

For
Sebastian Walsh
Ben Collins
Saul Pearson
Jack Hemingway

CONTENTS

Preface		9
Introduction. About This Book		13

SECTION I: THINKING ABOUT STEP-PARENTING

1	The Ten Principles of Step-Parenting	19

SECTION II: STEP-FAMILY LIFE

2	Getting Through the Day	53
3	Getting Through the Week	72
4	Discipline, Rewards and Punishments	93
5	Some Unpleasant Aspects of Step-Family Life	118

SECTION III: MAKING SENSE OF STEP-FAMILY LIFE

6	Understanding Step-Children	141
7	Understanding the Adults in Step-Families	167

SECTION IV: PRACTICAL INFORMATION

8	Legal Aspects of Step-Parenting	191
9	Sources of Help	197
10	Suggestions for Further Reading	201

Index		205

PREFACE

Step-parents are now common enough, but they do not enjoy much public esteem. Their relationships with their children are often assumed to be inevitably harsh and disfigured, poor imitations of 'natural' families. Yet step-parents are people who voluntarily take on a share of the care of another human being and make huge sacrifices of time and money to do it; they might well feel that they are entitled to respect and admiration as public benefactors. Instead, they have to put up with the widespread belief that you might as well hope to get the better of James Bond or Bugs Bunny as hope to be a successful step-parent.

There are, however, countless successful step-families in which children are able to develop to maturity in a secure and caring environment, and there is evidence to show that many grown-up step-children look back with affection and gratitude to what their step-parents did. It is my hope that this book will help a few step-parents, and potential step-parents, to join the successful number who are able to regard their achievements with pride, and whose children will feel glad to have known them.

This is not a 'step-parenting is fun' kind of book, however. Bringing up children is never a matter of unmitigated entertainment, and step-parenting is probably more difficult than 'ordinary' parenting—not least because, as a result of the losses and other upheavals that they have experienced, step-children are probably, on average, more difficult than other children. It is, though, an optimistic book, and I start from the assumption that the distinctive difficulties which step-parents encounter, over and above the routine difficulties of parenting generally, are all capable of being adequately resolved where there is enough goodwill and sense.

10   PREFACE

The distinctive difficulties, and rewards, of step-parenting occur in the area of personal relationships, and these are what this book is about. Practical child-care will be much the same whether the children are step-children or not—matters like colic, teething, building sand-castles, homework, pocket-money, shopping for shoes, and the general regime of barge-toting and bale-lifting that comprises family life. This does not mean that practical matters are unimportant. I shall argue that they are an important way—perhaps the most important one—for a step-parent to show care and affection for a child, and they are powerful influences in a family's emotional life in other ways. This is particularly so in step-families, where money and accommodation usually have more significance than they do in other households, and there can be no ignoring the influence that material conditions can have on a family's emotional well-being.

As well as discussing the rewards and troubles of step-family life, and suggesting ways of getting the best out of the situation and avoiding the pitfalls that beset you, I shall be discussing step-families and their experiences in general terms, in the hope that step-parents will recognise something of themselves and of their own experiences in what they read. Although there is no such thing as a 'typical' step-family, there is a common core of experience that all step-families share. One of the basic problems faced by step-parents is a feeling of isolation, a sense that they are alone in what sometimes seems a shameful situation. If readers are able to recognise themselves in this book, it may help to ease this isolation, and to make them aware that there are plenty of other people in the same boat.

Definitions and Limitations
The book is aimed primarily at people who are living full-time, or nearly full-time, with step-children. There are numerous variations on this basic version of a step-family, and the book would have become too unwieldy if I had attempted to cover them all. Step-children who come to stay at weekends or in school holidays, for example, introduce strains into the lives of the adults that are not

PREFACE 11

identical with those that come from living full-time with the children. The strains on a relationship that come from one of the partners setting aside a period of time each week to spend with children of a previous marriage are also distinctive, and the emphasis on step-children who are full-time should not be interpreted as meaning that I am indifferent to the problems of non-custodial parents. I have not given much space to the amalgamated family, that is, the household in which both adults have children from previous marriages, so that there are in effect two step-parents. I have also given no attention to homosexual households, though these may become increasingly common. I have given little space to the different experiences of men and women as step-parents, important though these obviously are. At the moment, the overwhelming majority of full-time step-parents are men, because it is still fairly unusual for a father to get custody of children in divorce settlements. This is changing, and the balance between step-fathers and step-mothers will presumably shift as more fathers get custody. Finally, I have had to ignore the huge range of possible time-scales in step-parenting. Some readers will find this book when their step-children are almost off their hands after years of care, and if such readers find anything to commend in the book, it might seem rather late to start making changes. Other readers may be just at the point of thinking about becoming step-parents—and if they are, I hope that they won't be put off.

On usage, I usually refer to a child as 'it', not because I think children are objects, but to avoid using the clumsy 'he or she' every time I need a pronoun. I use 'biological' for families that are not step-families, though the word strikes me as being a trifle clinical. I tend to refer to the adults' relationship within the household as a 'marriage', but this is for convenience, and covers any long-term domestic arrangement.

In writing this book, I have drawn on three main sources for ideas. The first is the considerable body of theory and information about families and their workings that is to be found in the social sciences, though I have tried to present this material in terms that are intelligible to readers who

12 PREFACE

have no training in these disciplines. Second, and undoubtedly more important, I have drawn from my own experience, as a step-father and as someone with a professional involvement with families that is now longer than I find it comfortable to acknowledge. Third, I have derived immeasurable benefit from the wisdom and advice of other people, and it remains to thank some of these.

Acknowledgements
My first, and most embarrassed, gratitude is to my stepsons, who will be only too well aware of the gulf between preaching and practice in our lives. I hope that they will not find this book too laughable. I have also learned something from the families with whom I have worked over the years, and I am grateful to them. Two old friends, Don Glen and Peter Hitch, have taught me much in innumerable conversations, some more sober than others, in East Anglian pubs and on Welsh hillsides. I have greatly benefited from discussions with Jack Greenwood, Judith Greenwood, Kelly Harvey, Bob Isgrove and Maggie Lancelot. I have not always accepted their advice, and any misjudgements and excesses are entirely my own responsibility. Finally, no words can express my gratitude to my beloved wife, Lorraine Hemingway.

Stephen Collins
Bradford,
Yorkshire,
June 1987.

INTRODUCTION—ABOUT THIS BOOK

This is a book for step-parents. Most of them hate the very word 'step' and use it rarely and reluctantly – though they are a group that is entitled to feel proud, rather than embarrassed, at having taken on the responsibility of someone else's children. It starts from the assumption that step-parenting is an interesting and potentially enjoyable experience, different from natural parenting but not necessarily less rewarding.

Step-parents meet the expectation of catastrophe at every corner. It crops up in the attitudes of your friends: 'And how,' they ask, dropping their voices solicitously, 'do you get on with little Gretel?' where Gretel is your step-daughter. They would not dream of asking such a question about your 'natural' children, and it would be a very odd thing if they did. 'Er, fine,' you answer lamely, immediately conscious of the row that you had with Gretel as she went off to the forest with Hansel that morning, and forgetting in your confusion that you had a similar unimportant row yesterday with another child who happens to be your 'own' rather than a step-child. When friends expect difficulties, it encourages step-parents to expect them, too, and if they are not careful they will find themselves attributing all the run-of-the-mill problems of family life to the fact that there is a step-parent there.

This book is an invitation to think about the whole business of step-parenting and how it might be possible to do it better. I am free with suggestions about how step-family life might be improved, but these suggestions are more in the form of ideas about step-parenting than advice on how to lead your life. I am not a great believer in advice, for in my experience there is a lot of truth in the old adage that wise people don't need advice and fools don't take it, and

14 INTRODUCTION—ABOUT THIS BOOK

in any case all step-families are different, and have to work out the solutions to their unique problems in their individual ways. You cannot do step-parenting with an instruction book in one hand (and perhaps the child in the other), but you have to think about it, and keep thinking about it.

How to Use this Book
The book is in four sections. The first, *Thinking about Step-Parenting*, sets out what I take to be the principles of being a step-parent—the attitudes and guidelines that seem to me to form a sensible basis for thinking about and doing the job of step-parenting. The second section, *Step-Family Life*, deals with the problems and challenges of step-family life—matters ranging from handling jealousy to sorting out finance and dealing with grandparents. The third section, *Making Sense of Step-Family Life*, contains ideas about what makes the various people in a step-family tick—and argues that it is helpful to try to understand this. The fourth section, *Practical Information*, gives a brief outline of the law as it relates to step-parenting, provides information about where step-parents might find help with their lives, and makes suggestions about further reading. Finally, there is an index designed to help the browser to find matters of particular concern.

Assumptions and Presumptions
The potential reader will perhaps have worked out that certain assumptions lie behind everything I have to say in this book, and in order that readers may make up their minds about how sensible these assumptions are, they need to be set out at this stage.

The first assumption is that normal family life is a process of imperfect survival, and that even the happiest families have their dark aspects. It is essential to bear this in mind if we are to keep the problems of step-parenting in proportion, and to avoid seeking unrealistically tidy solutions to untidy human problems. This does not mean that people should shrug and settle for domestic relationships that are unsatisfactory, much less that they should excuse their

INTRODUCTION—ABOUT THIS BOOK 15

own shortcomings in relationships as the inevitable consequence of imperfectible human frailty. The life of any family is certainly capable of being improved, but this will not happen if people get discouraged by setting their sights on an abstractly ideal family—which the chances are they would find extremely boring should they ever attain it.

Second, the fact that most families do not end in disaster, and are in practice acceptably successful, suggests that most problems are soluble given the sort of skill that families generate, and given adequate supplies of goodwill and good sense. I do not mean by this that all that is needed is cheery common sense, because family problems are distressing and a lot of family members are likely to feel that their feelings are being belittled if they are treated with hearty banter. But when a family is going through a particularly difficult patch, it may be important to remind oneself that most families have bad periods, and that usually they achieve some sort of solution at the end.

Third, families are, to adapt Le Corbusier's famous remark about houses, machines for living in. They are not mysterious or mystical objects of wonder, but places that exist to serve the needs of their members, and they work by processes that are highly complex but at least approximately comprehensible. The better these machines are understood, the better they will function, because the more efficiently they can be run. This theme is developed more fully in Section III.

The Rewards of Step-Parenting
If all goes well, step-parents can expect two distinct pleasures over and above those associated with natural parenting. The first is the deep satisfaction to be had from earning the love and trust of a child or young person who may have begun by treating you with resentment or suspicion, and who has finally become satisfied of your worth. Children who have always had their parents around impose no such probation and will not usually afford the deeply moving and proud moment when a parent realises that he or she has at last been accepted by the children. The second pleasure that step-parenting

16   INTRODUCTION—ABOUT THIS BOOK

offers is the chance to get to know the children much more intimately than usually seems possible with natural children. Meeting one's step-children when their personalities are at least partially formed makes a firmer basis for getting to know them and understanding them than having watched a smiling baby slip imperceptibly into adolescence and never having had reason to stop and ask what exactly it is that makes this child tick at this particular time—a question that is almost inevitably forced upon an incoming step-parent. Most adults are pretty convinced that their parents do not really 'know' them— perhaps because they feed their parents only highly edited accounts of their lives—and there is a potentially much better chance of real intimacy based on mutual understanding between step-parents and their children, because both will have engaged in a more formal and thorough process of getting to know the other than occurs in natural families. Intimate knowledge of another human being is one of the supreme pleasures of life, and the long acquaintance and shared experiences between step-parents and children offer a promising basis for such intimacy.

SECTION I

THINKING ABOUT STEP-PARENTING

1 THE TEN PRINCIPLES OF STEP-PARENTING

Like most important human activities, step-parenting needs a combination of experience, goodwill, good sense, luck, thought, care, time, trouble, skill, judgement—and any other human attribute you care to name. If that makes it seem daunting, then so it is, as is any action that involves responsibility for another human being. What is not possible, unfortunately, is to set out a few easy rules which, if you follow them carefully, will ensure success. Step-parenting is not like making a cake. There can be no simple handbook that will tell you what to do on any occasion, and when it comes to it, it is the step-parents' personal capacities that will decide how successful they are. But this does not mean that step-parenting is best carried out by blind instinct, relying on intuition and common sense and never sitting down to think out what might be going on in the household, or what effects your behaviour might be having. There are certain principles or guidelines that may make success more likely, and this chapter aims to define them, not as rules to be slavishly followed, but as things to keep in mind when working out how to go about the task of step-parenting that you have set yourself.

The principles of step-parenting are a mixture of two things: first, a series of what we may call 'dos' and 'don'ts', and second, a number of assumptions about how people are likely to get on best together. The two are not separable, and together give us ten points that I take to be the basis for good step-parenting—good in the sense of being helpful to the children and satisfying to the adults. These principles are:

1 Care can be as important as love.
2 Understanding is important.

20 STEP-PARENTS AND THEIR CHILDREN

3 Step-families are not inferior imitations of biological families.
4 Step-parents are not necessarily parents.
5 Personal relationships can hurt, but they can also heal.
6 Guilt can damage the health of the household.
7 Comparisons are odious.
8 Myths and superstitions have no place in a modern step-family.
9 Human emotions are seldom straightforward.
10 Parents are not just emotional caddies.

1 Care can be as Important as Love

Love involves a feeling of tenderness, and many step-parents never feel this for their step-children, or to nothing like the extent that they feel it for their biological children. Since they genuinely wish to love their step-children, this can lead to a sense of despair, for you cannot force yourself to experience this tenderness, which comes and goes in mysterious ways. What *can* be achieved by well-intentioned people who deliberately set out to do it is care—by which I mean looking after someone in a thoughtful and conscientious way and meeting their needs as fully as one can. Throughout this book we shall be looking for ways in which a step-parent can at once look after the children in this way, and demonstrate to them the extent of the step-parent's concern. Seeking to care for the children is a much more realistic hope than trying to induce a feeling of tenderness towards them, and in terms of a child growing up, care may be more important than love.

I am not, of course, suggesting that love, in the sense of feelings of tenderness, is not important, and if you do find that you have such feelings for your step-children, then both you and they are very fortunate. It is, however, obvious that there is more to bringing up children than feeling tender towards them. You have to change their nappies, take them to school, put up with their friends, bankrupt yourself on their behalf, live with their habits. Children keep you awake at night, they tear the wallpaper, ride their bikes over the flowerbeds, stuff your shoes down the lavatory, refuse to wear the lovely clothes you buy for

THE TEN PRINCIPLES OF STEP-PARENTING 21

them, eat unsuitable food, spill things, mend their motor bikes on the new carpet and treat you like dirt. Anyone who can sustain uninterrupted feelings of tenderness through all aspects of life with their children probably needs a brain-transplant. To supervise the development of a child towards some semblance of sociable adulthood requires an iron commitment, and in the process the feelings of tenderness that come and go are undoubtedly very important rewards, a source of psychological nourishment and energy when times are bad, but not in themselves enough.

I shall be returning to this theme at a number of points in the book, so for now all that needs stressing is that bringing up children is as much an exercise in care as in anything more mystical. It is sad that the noble word 'care' is in the process of becoming devalued, partly by a process of vulgar sentimentalisation in pop songs and children's comics, partly by being misappropriated by stony-hearted politicians who really care only about power. To care for someone is a most precious feature of our common humanity, and it is something that step-children, as well as every other child, need. You may not love your step-children in the sense of feeling tender towards them, you may not even like them very much, but you will be able to care for them, and that is important.

2 Understanding is Important
Understanding will not on its own solve problems, but it can help. If you understand the problems that beset you, it is often possible to dismantle them into their component parts, and when they are unpacked in this way, problems have a habit of looking less daunting. Your problem may be an awesome interlock of difficulties that threatens to overwhelm you, but taken to pieces may look like a series of lesser difficulties that can be tackled one at a time. Understanding things makes them less frightening, because fear breeds on mystery. If a step-family is in turmoil because the people in it are at each other's throats, it may be a very frightening place to be, and fear can only make matters worse; but if people have some grasp of why

22 STEP-PARENTS AND THEIR CHILDREN

relationships are so bad, then some of the fear will go out of the situation. And if you understand what is going on, you are less likely to respond unthinkingly and make matters worse by unconsidered retaliation. Your step-child may be behaving aggressively because it is insecure and angry, and is lashing out at the world in uncomprehending revenge. If you understand the child's behaviour, you will realise that it would be pointless to respond to aggression with aggression, so understanding may help you to control your temper and not respond to provocation.

Understanding a problem is not the same as solving it, but it is a start; so within a family, understanding what is going on is mainly a tool for making things happen and for generating change. Over and above the help of understanding in managing the daily life of a household, however, is the importance of understanding within personal relationships. There is good evidence that feeling understood is in itself highly beneficial, and that feeling misunderstood is destructive—for all that many of us luxuriated in the sense of being misunderstood when we were adolescents. Many people feel too embarrassed to say 'I understand' to someone in distress, but there is probably no more helpful thing on offer to that person than this sense of being understood. Being understood in this way can ease loneliness, so trying to understand someone is a form of making emotional contact with them. Trying to understand your step-children, therefore, is at once prudent, because it may suggest ways of handling them in more socially comfortable ways, and it is also a richly important means of caring for them.

Understanding usually makes for increased tolerance. 'To understand all is to forgive all' is an old maxim, in my experience usually uttered by maudlin drunks, but for all that, embodying an important insight and a common experience. In step-families, where there is often much to forgive, understanding can therefore be helpful. It is important, to be sure, to distinguish understanding from the making of excuses. I am, for example, genially forgiving of my own faults because I understand (or think I understand) what causes them and I suppose a purist might

THE TEN PRINCIPLES OF STEP-PARENTING 23

argue that my general behaviour might be improved if I were fractionally less tolerant—indeed, such a suggestion has from time to time been made. The habit of tolerating and hence excusing various forms of malefaction by attempting to explain them is the stock-in-trade of social scientists, but it merely serves to infuriate the rest of society. If, on the whole, in domestic matters, it is easier to put up with someone if one has some grasp, however rough and ready, of what makes him or her tick, such confusing of explanation and excuse can sometimes lead to trouble. Most people find that it is relatively minor acts and omissions by their domestic companions that cause them to reach for the carving knife, and such minor habits are often the most resistant to satisfactory explanations. To return to my own almost unblemished domestic practices, it is true that I occasionally fail to keep the place as tidy as some perfectionists might like—'pathological' is a word that has been rudely applied to this trivial shortcoming— but I have found from experience that the explanation that I offer in justification is regarded as too elaborate, not entirely convincing, and seems unaccountably to cause a deepening flush on the face of the person with whom I am having the discussion (or 'lecturing', to use her expression). I shall draw a veil over this distressing little domestic scene, but it serves to illustrate that there is an essential difference between understanding someone's behaviour and having that person explain it to you: the one improves tolerance, the other smacks of making excuses, and does not. To be useful, understanding must be an attempt to make sense of another person's behaviour and, so far as one succeeds, so will one's tolerance probably develop—and tolerance is one of the most useful domestic virtues.

Families are highly complex places, and the permutations of relationships within them are numberless and shifting. Understanding of the life of any individual family is bound to be imperfect, therefore, although what is going on within a household is often more intelligible to the people inside it than to someone on the outside. Often, however, the people in the household are so bound up in the fluidity

24   STEP-PARENTS AND THEIR CHILDREN

and the subtlety of the family's emotional life, the codes
and misunderstandings, the ups and downs and the whole
chaotic ethos, that they have lost the ability to make sense
of what is going on. When this happens, people can get
locked in patterns of relationships that are unpleasant but
which seem impossible to break out of. A step-parent, who
will often be slightly detached from the rest of the
household, however much he or she is bound up in its life,
may be well placed to introduce the understanding and
explanation that can break a destructive pattern. In other
cases, it may be sensible to seek outside help in making
sense of what is going on—and suggestions for finding
such help are given in Chapter 9. What is almost never
sensible is to assume that domestic life is too mysterious to
be understood, and to settle for a life of emotional reaction
and counter-reaction because you find the behaviour of
some or all the members of the household to be incomprehensible. Such a conclusion will block off all the helpful
powers of understanding that I have been describing.

As well as understanding the other members of the
household and how they relate together, step-parents will
do well to try to understand themselves and their attitude
to their circumstances. Throughout this book we shall be
identifying and discussing feelings and behaviour that are
not, if we are honest, very attractive. In the face of such
matters, and of the expectations of the outside world that
step-families are going to be hotbeds of emotional tribu-
lation, there are two responses that step-parents commonly
make, neither of them at all helpful, and both betraying a
lack of self-knowledge that comes from not trying to
understand oneself.

The first of these is denying that there are any
problems—which can end as an increasingly frantic insist-
ence that one's domestic life is trouble-free, that one sees
one's step-children as one's 'own', that one gets on better
with one's step-children than with one's 'own'; and the fact
that one of the step-children is in care, another is in
hospital and a third has disappeared is pure coincidence
because there are *no problems*. This account is, of course,
exaggerated, but it reflects an understandable human wish

THE TEN PRINCIPLES OF STEP-PARENTING 25

not to admit failure—or, more realistically, less then complete success. For a lot of step-parents are touchy about their situation, aware that everyone expects it to end in tears, convinced, or half convinced, that their relationships with the children are bound to be troublesome, and determined to prove the sceptics wrong, to overcome their own misgivings or, more admirably, to do a good job of what they have embarked upon with the children.

The trouble with this approach is twofold. First, it is almost certainly not true. Very few, if any, families are without problems, and the fact that many step-families are highly successful does not mean that this success was achieved without effort, and that there were no difficulties to be overcome on the way. The second is that in the effort to keep a cheerful face on things, the step-parent may have to ignore—or may fail to see—problems that would be easy enough to tackle once they were acknowledged. If you buy an expensive car you will be reluctant to accept that the knocking noise in the engine is anything important, and may decide to treat it as trivial and hope that it will go away. Only when the engine at last blows up will some people accept that there is a problem, whereas a pint or so of oil tipped into the engine at the outset might have solved the problem. So though denying that there are any problems may be a perfectly understandable way of approaching step-families, it may not be entirely sensible.

The opposite of denying problems is perhaps more common. It is to attribute *everything* that goes wrong in the household to the fact that it is a step-family. This emotional hypochondria looks for problems where none exist, exaggerates minor problems, and misunderstands normal events. If your teenage step-children are rude to you, it may be because they are poisonous adolescents, going through a normal phase of development in which they are starting to establish their independence from their family. This often involves assertive behaviour, which parents call rudeness but the teenagers put down to adult obtuseness. If a toddler kicks you, it is a mistake to assume that this is because you are an unsuccessful step-parent; more sensible to recognise that such behaviour is

26   STEP-PARENTS AND THEIR CHILDREN

common with toddlers and denotes little more than passing irritation. More substantially, perhaps, if a child really does get into difficulties—by needing psychiatric care, perhaps, or going to court—it is only too easy for everyone involved to lay much of the responsibility on the existence of step-relationships, and for a natural sense of guilt to beset the step-parent for presumably having failed the child. Almost certainly, however, the factors that have brought about the child's difficulties are numerous, and will include its personality and what happened to it before the step-parent arrived; so though the step-parent may well have contributed to the problems, it would be wrong to lay all the responsibility at his or her door. There is a good chance that things might have been a lot worse without the step-parent's presence.

Many step-parents seem to be able to perform the difficult trick of simultaneously denying any difficulties and practising this sort of emotional hypochondria. Logically, the two might be expected to exclude each other, but what seems to happen is that people are morbidly sensitive to difficulties in their step-families, although when they detect any, they recoil and deny that they have found anything. They may then pursue that denial to the bitter end, or they may quickly abandon it and exaggerate the importance of what they have found and their own part in it. Both denial and hypochondria are caused by a lack of confidence in what one is doing, and seem to improve with the passing of the years, as step-parents learn to live less on their nerves and to realise that they are doing an acceptable job and that minor failings are almost certainly not going to be catastrophic.

To bring together this rather long discussion of understanding, we can say that understanding is helpful to step-families because it helps to smooth their daily lives by making their problems look less frightening and hence more manageable, and to avoid unproductive responses to behaviour that will only get worse if it is wrongly handled. Trying to understand people is a way of loving them, because feeling understood is such a uniquely valuable benefit. Understanding increases tolerance of other people's

THE TEN PRINCIPLES OF STEP-PARENTING 27

behaviour, and when it is turned against oneself, it leads to self-knowledge that helps to discourage some unproductive habits of mind.

3 Step-Families are not Inferior Imitations of Biological Families

Step-families are based on different principles, and held together by different factors, from biological families. Biological families depend on certain widely held assumptions about the significance of blood relationships, and on the network of emotions and privileges that attach to kinship. These assumptions are so engrained that we never ask why a parent—particularly a mother—should care for a child, since that is what people do, and we are astonished and angry when they don't, or not very well. We assume that adults will care for their elderly parents, that brothers and sisters will be lifelong friends, and that relations take precedence over non-relations in all the important matters of life, from inheritance to who sits where at a wedding.

The importance of kinship is not to be underestimated, and the clear preferences that it involves are important to step-families. No doubt human kinship and all that it represents are based on the biological requirements of human children, who have a uniquely long period of dependence on adults, and so require a stable system of nurture if they—and the human race—are to survive. No doubt, also, kinship serves the needs of the economic system, for it has been crucial in concentrating wealth in a relatively limited number of hands, and has provided a basis for consolidating this wealth, and for passing it on from one generation to the next. But important as kinship is, it is not the only thing that binds human beings together; as well as the links of blood, human beings develop other ties, and it is to these that step-relationships belong.

Step-families come into being because of a series of decisions, of which a crucial one is that by the potential step-parent, that he or she is willing to take on a large share of the care of someone else's children. These decisions are often not made in very formal ways, and are arrived at by a

28 STEP-PARENTS AND THEIR CHILDREN

process of drift; but however haphazardly the choice gets made, it is quite different from the decision to start a biological family, where the decision to create children (again, often drifted into) is made on the basis of kinship and all the assumptions that go with it. In becoming a step-parent, one is cutting across these assumptions, and choosing to base the household on other factors.

Put briefly, step-families are held together by moral rather than emotional factors. They do not rely on the power of taken-for-granted affection in the way that many biological families do (with disastrous consequences in some cases). Step-families are, as I have said, based on a decision to care for someone else's children, and this is a decision that has strong moral overtones because it embodies assumptions about our obligations to other people. It is why step-parents are entitled to respect rather than the sort of suspicion that they seem almost invariably to attract, for they have voluntarily entered into a commitment to children, which is a commitment of supreme moral stature.

Morality is not perhaps an especially attractive term, for it has solemn overtones of good behaviour, and is heavily encrusted with pomposity. I am not suggesting that step-families are serious places with no emotional content. The commitment to the children is not usually made out of a po-faced sense of duty, and I should not like step-families to be thought of as consisting of nothing but joyless good behaviour, while biological families are full of affection and fun. What I want is to bring out, however, is that step-families are not simply imitations of biological families— and they are usually thought of as inferior imitations—but start from different assumptions and operate on distinctive bases.

Of these moral bonds holding step-families together, the most important is probably loyalty. This is a human quality of great importance. Loyalty is the characteristic that allows us to develop and sustain mutual obligations. When a step-parent takes on the responsibility of caring for the children, however it is decided that this care can best be carried out, what is being implied is a commitment no less

THE TEN PRINCIPLES OF STEP-PARENTING 29

than the one that biological children expect from their parents. A step-parent is agreeing not to abandon the children when the task becomes boring or difficult, or when the children are objectionable. The step-parent, just as much as a biological parent, hopes that the work of bringing up the children will be rewarding, but it is a one-way commitment in the sense that it is one that adults enter into without any similar commitment by the children —though sometimes, of course, they have been consulted. The responsibility is on the step-parent to see the commitment through, and to do this even if it is not rewarding. This is what I mean by loyalty—and it is obviously fundamental in providing children with the security that they need. Without this loyalty from the step-parent, there can be no serious prospect of the step-family getting under way as a working emotional unit, nor of the step-family surviving the inevitable stresses and strains of its early years.

What this means in practical terms is that it may be a mistake to try to think of one's step-family as if it were a biological one, and to hope to eliminate the differences both in one's own mind and in the way the household operates. It is clear that the reason why many adults enter second marriages is to try to recreate the environment of a 'normal' family, and it is perfectly understandable not to want to parade the 'stepness' of the household, and to hope that this quality will fade and the step-family become indistinguishable from a biological family. In many cases, of course, this is exactly what does happen, and the emotional environment of many step-families looks almost the same as that of most biological families. When this comes about without effort, well and good, but there can be high costs involved in trying to hurry the step-family into resembling a biological household. Among these costs can be a high level of pretence, and putting pressure on the children to repudiate parts of their lives that they might— especially when they get older—prefer to keep, such as their names, or their relationship with the biological parent who is no longer living with them.

Throughout this book, I use the terms 'family' and

30 STEP-PARENTS AND THEIR CHILDREN

'household' virtually interchangeably, and it would be perverse not to use the term 'step-family' when it is in almost universal use; but the distinctiveness of step-families should never be forgotten. For the most part the differences between step-families and biological families are a matter of degree—in that the problems that step-families encounter are much the same as those that biological families run up against. But the different moral basis of step-families, whether or not it gets translated into different emotional climates, seems to me to be a matter of pride for step-families, and something that they should not be too anxious to hide behind a mask of similarity with biological families. Commitment and loyalty are the attributes of mature and moral human beings, certainly no inferior to the less deliberate and more unconsidered factors that hold biological families together. Choosing to do something for someone else is better than doing the same thing just because it's the thing to do. Turning out on a winter's night to go to my step-child's school play, because I have chosen to make that sort of commitment to that child, is a more edifying reason than turning out from pride of ownership, or because it is expected, or because it never occurred to me not to. Step-families are not inferior copies of biological families, but human arrangements with their own distinct claims to respect and affection.

4 Step-Parents are not Necessarily Parents
Parenting brings together all sorts of different functions, and it may not be sensible for a step-parent to try to take them all on; better to choose a relationship with the children that could not be described as a purely parental one. It would, for example, be pointless to try to think in parental terms about a step-child who is virtually your own age, and it would probably be more sensible to think of yourself as a friend to step-children who are in their late teens. The children's views are crucial in this, of course, because no matter how much you may wish to be seen as a parent, if the children don't see it that way, you will be deluding yourself. In any case, the nature of a step-parent's relationship with the children is not static, but changes as

THE TEN PRINCIPLES OF STEP-PARENTING   31

they get older and as everyone in the household adjusts to one another.

None of the terms involved is precise, and though a word like 'parent' does not provoke a rush to the dictionary, it is certainly not easy to define simply. But granted that the language, and the roles that the language describes, are going to be vague, the possible relationships that a step-parent might have with the children are likely to be found somewhere between the two extremes of full parenting, and almost total uninvolvement. Clearly there will be a lot of overlap in the possible roles that a step-parent might consider adopting, and we are thinking about emphasis rather than hard and fast categories, but there are two broad possibilities available.

First, a parent, taking on the whole package of responsibilities and functions that this involves. Where the children are very young when the step-parent arrives, this may be the most appropriate role. When there is a previous parent still alive and in evidence, or where the children have memories of another parent, it would be sensible to consider whether such a wholehearted view of parenting is either possible or desirable. It could be that the children will not really believe in it, and that it could lead to all sorts of tensions and misunderstandings. I doubt if it could ever be right to *pretend* to be a child's biological parent; I doubt also whether any step-parent will altogether forget the 'step' part of the relationship, and a recurring theme within this book is that it is often not sensible to try to suppress the 'stepness' of the household. Wishing to become a parent to the step-children in as complete a sense of the term as possible may indicate a wish to be fully committed to them, and that is admirable; but it can also indicate a wish to force one's domestic life into as close a resemblance to a 'normal' family as possible, and that might not be wise. It could be that many of the problems of step-families could be avoided by a more cautious involvement by the step-parent and, in many cases, another role than that of parent might be prudent.

Second, a friend. This does not rule out caring, but it implies a more equal relationship than parenting. Friendship

32   STEP-PARENTS AND THEIR CHILDREN

deals in matters that are generally taken to be fairly easy
aspects of life, such as shared interests, spending spare
time together, and only discussing intimate emotional
matters or other private areas of a person's life by
invitation. Parenting, by contrast, takes for granted that a
child's private life is at least some concern of the parent,
and parents are inevitably concerned with the more heavy-
duty aspects of life, such as moral guidance, emotional
development and the like. Friendship is not a trivial
relationship, however, for it is quite capable of involving a
level of intimacy and a freedom that are unusual between
children and their parents; over a person's lifespan,
friendships may be as important in achieving happiness as
relationships with parents.

It is obvious enough that children need someone to be
involved in the aspects of parenting that I have just
described as 'heavy duty', but they also need—or will
greatly benefit from—having someone who takes an
interest in what they do, provides an acceptable level of
companionship, and in whom they can confide without
their confidences becoming entangled with the responsibilities that parents carry. A step-parent can provide a set
of emotional facilities for the children that are not usually
available from a parent, and this can mean that some step-
children are actually better off than their counterparts in
biological families, since they have a greater range of
relationships with adults available to them.

Some step-parents think of themselves as older brothers
and sisters to the children, but I am not sure how helpful an
idea this is. Being a brother or sister does not exclude any
caring aspects of a relationship with step-children, for
older brothers and sisters often carry a lot of responsibility
for the welfare of the younger children, but it implies a
more egalitarian relationship than parenting, and rules out
a number of aspects of full parenting. Brothers and sisters
do not usually punish younger children (nor, as I suggest in
Chapter 4, do most sensible step-parents), they do not have
any financial responsibility, and they are generally exempted
from taking a prominent role in teaching morality to the
children, inducing civilised habits and being involved in all

THE TEN PRINCIPLES OF STEP-PARENTING 33

the important decisions of their lives. Older brothers and
sisters can provide someone to learn the ways of the world
from, a relationship that is especially intimate because of
the amount of shared experience that it involves, and an
ally within the family conflicts. On the other hand, many
relationships between brothers and sisters are bitterly
competitive and antagonistic—and much of the point in
step-parents' pondering what their role in the household
might be is to avoid just these sorts of conflict. There is
another point, that a step-parent is not *really* a brother or
sister, so the role implies an element of make-believe that is
unnecessary if you are mainly concerned to develop an
egalitarian relationship with the children and avoid some
of the problems of adopting a parental relationship. If this is
the sort of relationship that seems appropriate, then it
makes sense to think in terms of being a friend, an
important form of relationship that avoids this element of
pretence and allows the children to have a less wholehearted
relationship with you, at least to start with, than the one
implied by the notions of brother and sister.

5 Personal Relationships can Hurt, but they can also Heal

We shall inevitably have a lot to say about the problems of
step-families, and shall discuss the ways in which things
can go wrong in step-family life, but there is another aspect
that should be stressed. No doubt some step-children are to
be pitied, the victims of step-parental neglect and jealousy,
but there are many others who owe much of their
happiness to their step-parent. There are plenty of cases of
highly successful step-parenting, where a child looks
successfully to its step-parent for the love and security
that it needs, perhaps is closer to its step-parent than to its
biological one, and is immeasurably better off in all aspects
of its life because of the step-parent. In such cases, a step-
parent may have put right some of the hurt and damage
that has come from the child's experiences. A child who is
left feeling insecure by the loss of a parent may slowly
recover its sense of security through the affection and
reliability of a step-parent. A child who blames itself may

34 STEP-PARENTS AND THEIR CHILDREN

learn to forgive itself, a child who is having trouble learning how to behave in acceptable ways may copy its step-parent and be taught by the step-parent the arts of social living. A child who is angry may be pacified, a child who is unhappy may learn to experience joy, a child who feels misunderstood or unloved may find a step-parent to understand and love it. A child who has been badly hurt may learn to trust adults again.

There is a long human tradition that the answer to much human distress is to be found in relationships with other human beings. We are a sociable species, and we need other people just as much as we need food and shelter. Small children run to their parents for comfort when they fall down or experience the catastrophic disappointments of childhood, and this continues throughout our lives. A warm and affectionate step-parent can provide this comfort and reassurance for children of all ages, and can do much to put right the legacy of pain from past losses and experiences, and to rekindle the prospect of happiness for the children.

Rather than dwell endlessly on the possibly destructive contributions made by a step-parent to the lives of children, by introducing the particular strains of step-family life with its jealousy and its guilt, step-parents and anyone concerned with step-families would do well to remember the healing potential of personal relationships, and look for ways in which step-family relationships can take on these healing capacities. There is, for instance, some research evidence that many step-children fare better in certain aspects of their lives than children of single parents, because of the step-parent's contribution as someone to identify with and to learn from. We shall be discussing this point further in Chapter 2; for now all we need to notice is that this example illustrates the essential principle that step-parenting has a potentially healing capacity.

6 Guilt can Damage the Health of the Household
Throughout this book we shall be discussing things that are nothing to be proud of—things like jealousy, anger, resentment, scapegoating, and numerous other manifes-

THE TEN PRINCIPLES OF STEP-PARENTING   35

tations of human unpleasantness. I shall be encouraging a frankness in acknowledging that some of these unedifying emotions are to be found lurking within oneself; but having accepted the existence of the sort of unlovely emotions that we shall be identifying as common in step-families—and in other families as well—the issue is what to do about them. It makes no sense to languish in horrified guilt at what you have recognised within yourself. Appalled honesty is one thing, disabling guilt is another. Perhaps you find yourself harbouring sexual desire towards your step-child: you do well to feel appalled, but the important thing is to ensure that these desires are not allowed to damage the child, and you are more likely to achieve that by realistic and clear-sighted planning than by allowing yourself to become paralysed by self-loathing.

There is a lot of guilt in step-families. The children sometimes think that their parents' first marriage broke up because of their behaviour. The biological parent is often beset by remorse at having disrupted the children's lives by the failure of the first marriage and the subsequent importation of a step-parent. The step-parent may be acutely conscious of the trouble that his or her arrival has caused, and of the unworthy feelings that he or she may have towards the children. Some of this guilt is appropriate, and I am certainly not arguing that what you do is of no importance and that you should effortlessly forgive yourself for everything. It probably does no harm at all for the biological parent to recognise the trouble to the children caused by the break-up of their parent's relationship, but it does start to do harm when that guilt comes to dominate the household, when remorse makes it impossible to say 'no' to the children, or stops you from ever seeking your own emotional satisfactions. Many wrong things may have happened in the history of the household, in the process of its being made and arriving at where it is today, but when these things are past mending they should not be allowed to jeopardise the future.

It is because guilt can translate into actions and attitudes that hurt the children that it needs to be controlled. A proper sense of mortification at the trouble you have caused

36 STEP-PARENTS AND THEIR CHILDREN

them may be appropriate and deserved, and might make you more careful in future, but guilt can also be demoralising and rob you of the energy and resilience that you need for coping with children on a day-to-day basis, to say nothing of coping with emergencies or other dramas. Guilt can lead to depression, and where it entails punishing oneself for what makes one feel guilty, it can be notably self-destructive. But as well as what guilt does to you, it can also affect how you treat the children. One likely consequence of guilt is to treat them with an excessive level of protectiveness. The implicit argument seems to be that because I have caused these children so much pain, then I must strive even harder than other parents to protect them from harm. Obviously children must be protected from harm, but there comes a point at which protection becomes stifling, and the child's safety is only secured at the cost of restricting its growth into independence. Taking risks is an essential part of growing up, and these risks are both emotional and physical—being prepared to take risks in a relationship is the only way to fulfil its potential, and taking calculated physical risks is the only way of learning one's body's potential and limitations. Over-protectiveness is a common fault in step-families—understandable, but not good for the children.

For all that it is often appropriate, guilt is commonly thoroughly unproductive, rooted in irrational prejudices, and representing a disproportionate chastisement for offences that are imaginary or unimportant. Guilt is implanted early in our lives, and at once embodies and reinforces the system of what is right and proper of the people who do the implanting—most usually our parents, though they in turn are articulating the system of values of the society of which they are a part. Not all guilt is 'inherited' from our parents, but the basic psychological structure is laid down in the nursery—or whatever the modern counterpart of a nursery may be. So when we are guilty, we are punishing ourselves for having let our parents down, and we need to remind ourselves that we are no longer in the nursery, that our parents' values were theirs, and expressed the standards of a different time in

THE TEN PRINCIPLES OF STEP-PARENTING 37

history, which may not suit our times or make sense to ourselves as rational adults. A lot of people think that sex is dirty, and this effectively stops some of them enjoying it. Perhaps they learned this view of sex from their parents who had it in turn from theirs; and so we may find some antique moral system obstructing our lives simply because nobody has stopped to ask whether we need this particular fossil value before passing it down the generations. Identifying how irrational such a view of sex really is will not in itself open the doors to sexual pleasure, but it will at least make a start in deporting irrational ideas from our lives, and restricting the killjoy potential of guilt.

In step-families, it makes sense to examine one's own guilt from time to time and decide what triggers it off, then go on to consider whether that behaviour is reprehensible according to rational standards, or only according to a set of moral assumptions that have lain about in one's mind for years without being questioned, but which have no real validity in the world as we now occupy it. I am always guilty when I don't finish a meal, because as a child during the Second World War food was scarce and I was aware how lucky I was to have any, in contrast to the starving children of eastern Europe. I learned to feel that I was in some way letting these children down by not eating something that they would have been so glad to have. As an adult who unsuccessfully struggles with a tendency to get fat, this guilt is not just irrational but actually self-destructive. Many step-parents feel guilty because they do not love their step-children. If you accept that love is not something over which you have much control, then there is little point in feeling guilty. If, however, you catch yourself neglecting your step-children, or treating them worse then your own biological children, then this is something over which you have some control, and guilt might be appropriate (provided it leads to some tangible improvement).

Step-parents have much to be proud of—taking on the responsibility of other people's children is a valuable human act that should be rewarded. Perhaps you do not think that you are making such a good job of it as you

38 STEP-PARENTS AND THEIR CHILDREN

would like, but that may be because your own standards are very high, rather than because you are really not succeeding. So the guilt comes in, but the merits of self-forgiveness could be sensibly pleaded. If, instead of feeling permanently guilty, you stop periodically to ask yourself where your standards came from and whether they are the right ones, then you might find that you are asking an impossible amount of yourself, and that actually you are not doing too badly. One way of doing this is to imagine how a well-intentioned person outside the household might see things; would that person see an adult acting with kindness and thoughtfulness towards the children? So why should your conscience be so much more critical than the well-intentioned observer? I spend much of my time talking with step-parents, and they seem completely unable to recognise the achievements in what they are doing for the children, which are obvious to everyone else, and chronically disposed to guilt for not achieving their ideal—which is probably impossible, and certainly immeasurably higher than the standards that biological parents set for themselves.

Certainly there will be failures, times when guilt and apology are fully appropriate, and where the step-family brings out the worst in people; but it is not inconceivable that you are doing well enough in other areas of stepparental life, and you might consider celebrating your successes rather than being so hard on your failures. A periodic cleaning out of your conscience, to see how useful is the moral lumber stored in it, may be a better way of being a parent than spending your life in remorse.

Guilt is a complex emotion. There is little doubt that it is the source of a lot of emotional energy: many of the good things in the world come to be there because someone's guilt caused them to want to do something about poverty or illness or injustice. Some religions thrive on their promise to shift the debilitating burden of guilt, and we are inclined to class people as mentally ill if they do not seem to suffer from as much guilt as the rest of us. Against the creative possibilities of guilt, though, must be set its potential destructiveness, its capacity to lead to depression and inertia, and an inability to find pleasure. A lack-lustre life bedevilled by guilt is no basis for bringing up children.

7 Comparisons are Odious

Faced with incessant invitations to expect trouble, many step-parents make things harder for themselves by setting their circumstances alongside an idealised view of family life, and get even more disheartened by the comparison. This idealised image of the family depicts a married couple in soggy domestic contentment, with a tribe of pretty children of neatly graded sizes playing joyfully and tidily together, with perhaps a cat slumbering on the geometric centre of the fireside rug. Readers who live like that, or who want to, should proceed no further with this book: they will not enjoy it. On the other hand, readers whose domestic relationships are less orderly, whose children are more likely to be quarrelling than playing co-operatively and whose cat normally spends its time shredding the furniture and uses the hearthrug for purposes other than sleep, may find the image of family life embodied in this book recognisable. This temptation to make unrealistic comparisons is particularly important for step-parents who have no children of their 'own'. Many, probably most, parents are well aware of the murderous rage that their children can induce, the feelings towards the children that they would prefer not to acknowledge, and which are so different from their normal emotions. A step-parent who has never experienced this could be forgiven for feeling appalled when shaken by a particularly vehement wave of anger or antagonism, and for confusing such feelings with being an unsatisfactory parent, but this can cause accumulating damage to confidence and morale. It is not, to be sure, admirable to get so enraged by one's children, any more than it is to allow an affection that is dangerously near to sexual desire to develop for them, but the point about such unacceptable feelings towards children is that they need recognising and controlling; they should not be allowed to form the basis of demoralising guilt. A step-parent who questions his or her competence as a parent

40 STEP-PARENTS AND THEIR CHILDREN

needs to know that such inappropriate feelings are common in relationships between biological parents and children, and are not peculiar to step-parenting. I take it for granted in this book that families are on the whole a good thing—though they certainly don't suit everyone; but they are places of eddying emotion and ambiguous satisfactions, demanding a high price—commercially and emotionally— for membership, quarrelsome as often as contented, where competition for the lavatory is a commoner feature than family outings and breakfast is a sullen occasion.

Real families, in other words, muddle along. This muddling along should not, by the way, be underestimated, for parents pick up an extraordinary level of capability and knowledge which they bring to bear on family difficulties, and children rapidly acquire a remarkable range of domestic and social skills, as anyone who has been comprehensively outwitted by a two-year-old will know; but though families are highly sophisticated social organisations, and for the most part competent (and wise), there can be no denying that they present a rather ramshackle aspect to the tidy-minded, and that there is a temptation to confuse such ramshackleness with incompetence. But there is no sense in getting disheartened by comparing the untidiness of one's own family relationships with some non-existent ideal. No doubt in your family there are tensions and difficulties, periods of unhappiness and anger, ill-tempered mealtimes, jealousies and hatred, of ignoring and being ignored, but so there are in lots of families, and all this does not necessarily occur because the family is a step-family; it is a mistake to attribute the normal ups and downs of family life to a supposed cuckoo in the nest. Certainly, the original family, as it existed before the step-parent arrived, may have come to grief—probably will have done, since most step-relationships are now the result of divorce rather than death: and certainly the experience of having come to grief once is likely to affect the family's confidence in its ability to cope in future, but it does not help to compare one's own inglorious reality with the ideal family with the pretty children and the orderly cat.

THE TEN PRINCIPLES OF STEP-PARENTING 41

8 Myths and Superstitions have no Place in a Modern Step-Family

Before even beginning to sort out the difficulties in their own lives, step-parents have to deal with the general hostility that their situation attracts and which has the effect of making real difficulties worse by demoralising people and sapping their confidence. I have suggested that step-parents are highly prone to a species of emotional hypochondria: the magnification of minor episodes or comments into imaginary catastrophes. A small child may say to its step-parent, 'I don't like you'; such a common, perhaps universal, expression of passing irritation is not taken not seriously in most families, but to a step-parent, only precariously confident in his or her relationship with the child and fully prepared to find difficulties, the child's idle remark may be deeply wounding. If the cold light of reason is turned on such a reaction, of course, it seems absurdly exaggerated and the parent's reaction foolishly touchy, but such is the freight of bad association that has become attached to step-parenting that step-parents are encouraged to look for difficulties—and in human relationships, expecting difficulties is a guaranteed way of finding them.

The fundamental question that has to be answered is whether there is something in step-parenting that inevitably brings out the worst in people. To put the same question another way: does the bad press that step-parents get embody centuries of experience of badly-behaved step-parents or is it baseless superstition? Only be attempting to answer these questions can the pall of gloom and malevolence that hangs over step-parenting be dispersed and people allowed to get on with sorting out their lives without discouraging distractions.

We meet the wicked step-parent when we are very young and impressionable. Generally it is the step-mother who behaves so badly in fairy stories and at whose behaviour we are encouraged to hiss (in a display of ill-manners that is actually encouraged by adults) in panto-mime. Later, perhaps, we meet the charmless Mr Murdstone, bitten by David Copperfield, and getting no

42 STEP-PARENTS AND THEIR CHILDREN

more than he deserved, and later, almost certainly, we meet Hamlet, patron saint of step-sons, tipped off about what a horror his step-father is by his own father's ghost. So it is perhaps not surprising that people distrust step-parents when they are first introduced to them as the stock-in-trade of nursery villainy, in company with ogres and wicked witches, and continue to run into them in what they read later in life.

The difference, of course, is that most people lose interest in ogres and wicked witches fairly early in their lives, presumably because such villains have no counterparts in the real world, while evil step-parents continue to crop up in adult literature. If wicked step-parents were confined to fairy stories, they would probably not trouble us. We do not take much account of the rest of the fictional events in fairy-tales. People do not order their lives on the basis of godmothers with magic powers or pumpkins turning into stagecoaches, and I'm not sure that I have ever met a footman, let alone one who turns into a mouse at midnight. 'You have to kiss an awful lot of frogs before you find a prince', runs a famous piece of graffiti, a reminder that the plots of fairy stories haven't much in common with our daily lives—in which, incidentally, most people do not live happily ever after. If that were all there was to it, step-parents could even take some comfort from their treatment in fairy-tales, where they share the stage with, for example, toads, handsome and blameless creatures that are just as libellously represented as step-parents.

Matters become more complicated because of the importance that is sometimes placed on fairy stories by suggesting that there may be more to them than juvenile entertainment. Fairy stories are, by this argument, immensely ancient myths that served the purpose of helping our ancestors to manage the dark passions with which they were shaken. Telling stories acts as a release for the tensions of primitive societies because the act of telling them creates a sense of distance and an objectivity that makes them manageable. On this line of argument, step-parenting could be seen as the site of certain elemental passions, and the occurrence of wicked step-parents in

THE TEN PRINCIPLES OF STEP-PARENTING 43

fairy stories would at once be a demonstration that the problems of being a step-parent belong to the rawest aspects of our humanity; the stories are supposed to be a means of preventing our forebears from being overwhelmed by the naked malevolence of step-parenting.

Whether or not fairy stories have any such function as a safety valve for the destructive lusts of primitive society seems to me to be open to question—and it is also open to question whether our human predecessors were really such an especially unattractive bunch as they seem, according to this argument. What is fairly clear, however, is that step-parents were for the most part grafted onto fairy stories fairly recently, and that the wicked step-parent of fairy-tale is not some antique figure howling its message from savage prehistory. Far from being such a disgraceful fossil, step-parents seem to have been used by the Brothers Grimm in order to clean up the folk stories that they collected from German peasants in the early nineteenth century. These stories were indeed full of primitive vice—matters like incest and infanticide—that the Grimms judged far too strong for the taste of the urban readership for whom the tales were being retold. By re-defining, for example, Hansel and Gretel's mother as a step-mother, infanticide (which is not unknown in societies that lack contraception) becomes comprehensible and less 'unnatural'. Step-parents, in other words, were a literary device to sanitise genuinely ugly aspects of the human condition with which they originally had little connection.

Modern empirical research bears out the probability that the wicked step-parent of folklore is no more substantial than the fairy godmother or talking fish. Careful comparisons between step-families and similar biological families have consistently failed to show step-families as noticeably more unhappy or otherwise troubled. While there is little doubt that step-children are over-represented among the victims of child abuse, it seems likely that these tragic victims often live in households where there are other destructive features, such as severe poverty, or a parent with chronic difficulties in sustaining relationships, and that it is these features, rather than the 'stepness' of

44 STEP-PARENTS AND THEIR CHILDREN

the household, that are largely to blame. In well-established households, where the step-parent has made a commitment to caring for the child, most research studies have found few significant differences, and there is certainly nothing in the research to support the fairy-tale tradition of step-parental cruelty. Some references to the research will be found in the final section of this book on further reading, if readers wish to pursue the matter.

If there is any historical substance in the wicked step-parent, it almost certainly lies in social conditions that need not trouble us because they have long-since vanished. There is no doubt that step-parenting has been, historically, a common arrangement. As life expectancy has increased, so the number of young widows and widowers has fallen, and the proportion of step-children has fallen with it, picking up in this century when divorce replaced death as the main reason for parentless children; but what went on in these step-families of past time is not at all clear. In the very meagre record we have of people's experience of step-parents in the past, one theme stands out, and that is the question of inheritance. In the common pattern of inheritance, the eldest son was left everything, so it is not hard to work out why step-children might have been unwelcome. If you were the second wife of a rich man, all his wealth would be inherited by his son by his first wife, your step-son, and your children would get nothing. With such high stakes, and in a world where violence was a recognised way to get what you wanted, a spot of judicious neglect or ill-treatment might well remove the step-child, and leave the way clear for your son to inherit—and presumably do something to protect your own future.

We no longer live in such a world. People do not nowadays leave everything to the eldest son, and ordinary people do not poison or strangle anyone who gets in the way of their ambitions. Nor, it is probably true to say, did ordinary people in the past. Such behaviour was confined to the very rich and powerful—and for the most part the daily experiences of ordinary people in the past have slipped into oblivion, since only the lives and emotions of the rich were thought worth recording. It is a mistake,

THE TEN PRINCIPLES OF STEP-PARENTING 45

therefore, to assume too easily that the sort of problems that modern step-families experience go back to time immemorial. All sorts of things have changed, and step-parents should not be too oppressed by the persistence of the wicked associations of their role. There is reason to be sceptical that these associations embody the record of inevitable malice, the inescapable unleashing of the nastier elements in our nature brought on by the proximity of step-children. For the most part we are dealing with baseless folklore or the leftovers of an obsolete social system, and these should be allowed to do no more than caution us that there presumably have been bad step-parents and that we may need a deliberate effort if we are to behave better than the villains of fairy-tale and fiction.

For the children, the wicked step-parent can be expected to contaminate real relationships, at least in the early stages of their life with a step-parent, when there is almost bound to be an element of fantasy about step-parental wickedness. This is probably true whatever the child's age, though the quality of the fantasy will clearly vary greatly according to age. But children are in general pragmatic people, and half-formed ideas about step-parents culled from fairy stories will be unlikely to survive the experience of an affectionate and courteous adult, so it is probably not sensible to be too preoccupied with how a child might think about step-parents in general. This does not mean that a child's ideas should be belittled or dismissed, and it is obviously important to try to understand them and to respect them; but it might be a mistake to be too assertively on your best behaviour, just to show the children that you are not the wicked individual of folklore. That would be likely to end with the children adding deviousness to the catalogue of your shortcomings when your mask finally slips. A sensible adult behaving acceptably is a far more effective counter to the myth of wickedness than a conspicuous demonstration of niceness.

9 Human Emotions are Seldom Straightforward
I take it for granted that most human emotions are mixed.

46   STEP-PARENTS AND THEIR CHILDREN

You may be wholeheartedly devoted to your family, but still harbour a suppressed resentment at the time and trouble it requires. You may love your child, and be almost permanently angry with it, so that tenderness and rage give place to each other with alarming speed. There is no need to pile up examples: most of us live with the fact of mixed emotions—we have to, since they seem to be an inescapable part of being human—but step-families, perhaps more conscious than most of the negative bits of feeling that creep in, need reminding that it is possible to harbour conflicting feelings towards someone. There is nothing unusual or unhealthy in this fact, so it should not be allowed to become a source of guilt. The problems start when one is on the look-out for bad feelings—indifference, dislike, hostility—because there is little doubt that you will find them, but you may in the process miss the positive feelings that go alongside them. When a child hurts itself, there may be a whisper of pleasure within your immediate concern, and you may hate yourself for it—ignoring the genuineness of the concern, or the comfort that the child has gained from you. All the emotions that we shall be discussing in this book are ambiguous in this way, and it is as well to accept that this is a fact of life, rather than become too preoccupied with the bad elements in our feelings. We wish these were not there, but they may exist as a necessary part of the good bits that we are pleased about. The mixture within emotions is not usually evenly balanced and normally one part will dominate: tenderness may be the dominant element in your feelings towards a child, for all that there is anger embedded in the tenderness. But it follows that it is crude and pointlessly unrealistic to classify emotions as being simply good or bad, since most of them are both.

This tendency to split emotions into their good and bad components can take the form of an exaggerated wish to avoid all forms of conflict within the household, because such conflicts trigger off feelings that one would prefer not to acknowledge. The domestic quarrel is perhaps the most neglected aspect of daily life. There has been some attempt to study it in its extreme version of domestic violence, but

THE TEN PRINCIPLES OF STEP-PARENTING 47

it is obvious that most domestic rows are in a different universe from the brutal attacks that leave children and women terrified and wounded. There may or may not be a continuous link between that sort of savagery and the household tiff, though I rather doubt it, but what is important to recognise is that quarrels are normal, and not in themselves a sign of any serious defects in relationship. There are some people who regard an absence of quarrels as more worrying than their presence—a British social services department attracted widespread derision a few years ago when it refused to approve a couple as potential adopters on the grounds that they never quarrelled and that their relationship was therefore an unhealthy one. The thinking behind this is that it is better to express anger than to suppress it, because if it is hidden it will rankle and find its outlet in other ways; a lot of people believe that it is better to vent your feelings in a row than to bottle them up. Some couples stop quarrelling when they lose interest in each other, and by the same token some couples are able to express their love only aggressively.

In step-families, then, quarrelling is not in itself something to get too bothered about. It might be nicer if everyone lived together in placid harmony, but what psychologists call a high level of expressed emotion and everyone else calls throwing crockery does not in itself spell out anything particularly ominous, and should not be interpreted as a sign that the household is lapsing into misery, nor that an angry step-parent is necessarily a cruel one. Obviously quarrels are sometimes the start of a process that is going to end in disaster, but one should give oneself the benefit of the doubt and refuse to take rows any more seriously than biological families usually do.

The background is that many people in step-families have experienced an unhappy domestic life that ended in broken relationships, so they have at once higher hopes and more reason to fear the worst in their new household. Where the previous household broke up in shouting and anger, a row in the new household may seem depressingly reminiscent of what has gone before, and come to be feared as a prelude to things going wrong in exactly the same

48 STEP-PARENTS AND THEIR CHILDREN

way—with, perhaps, a resolve not to let one's anger out,
which may not be a very sensible resolve. The rows in the
new household may be the start of the rerun of an old
script, but it is important to remember that the people are
different, and so is the relationship between them; the
children are older, and at a different stage of development,
which means that their squabbles with each other and with
their adults will be different in meaning and content.

10 Parents are not just Emotional Caddies

The last principle is that parents and step-parents are not
mere emotional caddies for their children. Families are by
their nature mainly agencies for child-rearing, but it does
not follow that parents have no right to expect that there
should be something in family life other than the rather
bloodless satisfaction of a job well done when their children
are at last launched as adults without anything too
catastrophic happening, or at least nothing that can be
blamed on the parents. Parents, and particularly step-
parents, have put themselves to a lot of trouble on behalf of
their children, and are entitled to their share of the
satisfactions and pleasure of family life, and that means
their share of the courtesy. Courtesy, like all versions of
love, stands a high chance of going unrequited, but as an
element in successful personal relationships it is only going
to work if it is a two-way process. Children are not, on the
whole, especially solicitous of their parents' needs—
though they are often very good at knowing what will
make their parents uncomfortable and how far it may be
safe to go; but it is usually necessary to teach them that
parents are human beings of the same status and concerns
as theirs. This will, of course, be dismissed as nagging and
will often bear a depressing resemblance to the 'treating
this house like a hotel' routine that many of us went
through with our own parents, but it is preferable to being
treated as a doormat and feeling like a waste product. It is
particularly important for families with a step-parent in
them to be kept aware of the rights of parents, for such
families often contain a lot of guilt, and with step-parents
demoralised by their vilified role there can easily develop a

THE TEN PRINCIPLES OF STEP-PARENTING 49

nervous passivity in the face of children's overwhelming assumptions of their own importance in the family. In practice, plaintively telling your children that you are a human being, too, is not likely to be very effective, and you will probably do better to assert it in more tangible ways, like insisting that you as well as the children get a second go when you throw a six at Ludo because you are sick of losing all the time, or refusing to drop everything because a witless teenager has missed a bus and wants a lift to a party (and at the other end of the evening cutting up rough when you are got out of bed to pay a taxi fare incurred by the same witless teenager whose assumption of your invariable good nature has become enhanced by a beneficent alcoholic glow).

SECTION II

STEP-FAMILY LIFE

2 GETTING THROUGH THE DAY

A Machine for Living In
In the Introduction I described families as machines for living in. What I meant by this was that families exist for the purpose of serving the people who live in them, and that they are capable of being made to work better by well-informed tinkering. This chapter is about what the purposes of step-families are, and how step-families might be tinkered with to make them run better.

When starting out on any major project, it is mere common sense to be clear about where one is going and how one proposes to get there. Bringing up a family is the major undertaking in many people's lives, yet most of us embark on it with only the vaguest idea of what it involves and tackle it with little clear direction. People learn parenting on the job, and in most cases this rather haphazard approach works well enough, so that most children make the hazardous journey to maturity with hardly a scratch to show that their parents hadn't a clue about what they were doing when they decided to start a family. In the business of learning to be a parent, the main and the best teachers are not the writers of child care books, but the children. From the first attempts to account for a newborn baby's whimpers, parents learn from their children, and the craft of parenting is learned bit by bit, gaining confidence as people gain experience.

Because step-parents take on children who are already some way into their lives, the opportunies for learning parenthood from the children are reduced, and the children will already be involved with their adults in forms of relationship which have been negotiated in the hit-and-miss process of child-rearing that went on before the step-parent arrived. Since the chances are that at least some

54 STEP-PARENTS AND THEIR CHILDREN

aspects of these relationships are not what you would like, there is often a sense that step-parents are stuck with someone else's mistakes—which may lead to a temptation to introduce a regime that will get the children behaving more as one would wish, and point their lives in directions that their step-parent would prefer. I take it that most step-parents have the sense to resist this temptation. Most biological parents learn early on that it is well-nigh impossible to get children to do in life what one would wish, and to get them to behave exactly as one would like—or only at an unacceptable cost. Parenting involves helping children to lead their own lives, not in writing the script for them. A new step-parent may accept all that, and be determined not to impose his or her own standards and expectations on the children, but that does not answer the question of what on earth one is to do with these children. What, in other words, does bringing up children entail? What is one aiming to do? What are the principles of it all? Can one hope to do more than simply get through each day without unpleasantness?

The easiest part of bringing up children is to define the task in general terms—like allowing them to achieve their potential, or to fulfil their individuality. Unfortunately, such manifestos are not much help when facing the sort of situations that form the texture of domestic life. James proposes to watch television instead of doing his homework. Lucy intends to spend the night at a party with some young people who would not be one's own first choice as suitable companions for her. John has transferred the entire contents of the refrigerator to the washing machine and is now pulling the cat's tail. In such circumstances, general statements about individuality and potential are rather less use than a handy bottle of gin—especially as Lucy has now appeared in her proposed costume for the said party, which turns out not to be the sort of thing that any daughter of mine . . . There are, of course, people who believe that any control will stunt children's emotional growth, and that bringing up children involves removing any limits to their exploration of the world. On this argument, James should be left to his television, Lucy to her unsuitable friends and

GETTING THROUGH THE DAY 55

semi-nudity, and John should be actively encouraged in his creative transfer of things from fridge to washer, and be allowed to maim the cat if that is what he wants to do. The problem with such a view is that the emotional growth of the children is achieved at the expense of the emotional survival of the parents. A related problem is that children brought up in such a regime may be as creative and fulfilled as anything, but are effectively disqualified as participants in the real world. Bringing up children, therefore, involves balancing the demands of creativity and self-actualisation against the demands of keeping approximately sane and preparing to live in an adult world that is ill-disposed towards people it regards as undisciplined and unsocialised.

Meeting Needs

This chapter, then, sets out to define what the fundamental tasks of being a step-parent are—and what the tinkering with the domestic machine might be aimed towards. I am not proposing a schedule of rules, nor a list of objectives, because children cannot be brought up with a rule book. It is a business of perpetual negotiation, rather than the imposition of parental wishes. Rather than list rules and objectives, therefore, a better approach would be to set out what the various family members need from the family— and to take it for granted that families exist to meet these needs. In practice, of course, the children's needs take priority in most households, so the bulk of this chapter will be about what children need from the adults in their lives, and how those adults can meet these needs. Adults' needs, however, are neglected at peril. Since so many second marriages fail—which include a lot of marriages involving step-children—it is apparent that many people involved in second marriages are not finding that their own needs are being met. This may be because these needs are commonly being forced to take a back seat in favour of those of the children, for it is clear enough that a step-parent who is prepared to shelve his or her own emotional and practical requirements in order to attend exclusively to those of the step-children, is asking for trouble. The needs of children will be better met by adults who are contented, which

56 STEP-PARENTS AND THEIR CHILDREN

means that their own needs are not being entirely neglected in favour of the children's. This probably requires that the parents take the trouble—usually a conscious decision—to manage the household so as to leave some space from caring for the children to look after their own needs.

Needs are not the same as wishes. I wish I had a big fast car: I do not need a big fast car, because I can get along perfectly well without one (in fact, because of the way I drive, probably much better). I do need food and shelter, because I cannot survive without them. But there is an important fuzzy area in which it is not clear whether something is a need or a wish. It is possible to survive without a television set, though for many people a television is virtually a necessity because life would be unthinkable without one. You cannot, in other words, simply define needs in basic biological terms, because there are important social elements involved in determining what is seen as a necessity. Many step-children would no doubt wish that their biological parents had never split up, but they did, and the child's needs remain and must be met in new ways. And of course, different members of a household will have different versions of what is necessary —or even essential. Teenagers may decide that a motor bike is a need because all their friends have them (or are trying to persuade their parents that all their friends have them). Because conformity with their contemporaries is important for many teenagers, a wish becomes translated into a need. One person's need is another person's luxury, in other words, and it is wise not to dismiss one's children's aspirations as mere frivolity. Adults would do best to cast their minds back to their own childhood, to recall the intensity of desire for something and the unreasonableness of their parents' refusal, before deciding too casually that a child's demands are unimportant.

All a child's needs, however defined, can probably never be met in full, and bringing up children is a matter of recognising that there are going to be inevitable short-comings. It makes sense, therefore, to try to arrive at a working list of needs that must be met if a child is to develop emotionally and physically. It also makes sense to clarify in your own mind what the step-parental regime is intending to accomplish, and this is most usefully done in terms of defining the children's needs. But before going on to try to describe what children need from their families, and how these needs can be met, there is a final general point on the wishes/needs distinction that should be made. The intensity of a child's desire for something does not, obviously, convert that desire into a need, though it should certainly make the adults stop and think before dismissing it out of hand; but in deciding what desires of a child should be met, it is worth remembering that a lot of biological parents of step-children are beset by guilt that the failure of their relationships has possibly damaged the children, and this makes such parents prone to over-indulgence as an atonement for their own guilt. Step-parents are sometimes so preoccupied by the image of the wicked step-parent that they may be excessively indulgent in order to demonstrate that they are not in the traditional mould. In both cases, shrewd children will spot a vulnerability as they go about the routine childhood task of manipulating their parents, so adults in step-households need clearer heads than most as they try to define and meet their children's needs. This chapter is intended to help them to set priorities and approach the task in a sensible way.

The Needs of Children
Children need admiration and stimulation. Step-parents can provide these and create an atmosphere that embodies them, just as well as a biological parent. Stimulation encourages children to explore the world and to develop their capacities for living in it. It helps children to feel alive and to take creative risks, as well as to do 'well' in school and at work. Admiration is the basis for a sense of worth. If we are secure in our own belief in ourselves as worthwhile and lovable people, then we can withstand most of the disappointments and pain that life inevitably brings, but a sense of worth is not a fixed attribute, acquired at our mother's breast, and with us for the rest of our lives as a

58 STEP-PARENTS AND THEIR CHILDREN

permanent armour against fate. Most people probably first acquire it very early on in life, but it is liable to fall into disrepair if it is neglected, and can be battered to destruction by events. It needs attention and renewal, for even the most robust sense of worth is never complete or without fragility. Where it is lacking, it can often be implanted, and where it has been destroyed, it can often be replaced. People get their sense of worth from many sources—work, for example, or alcohol or religion—but for most people their sense of worth comes from their personal relationships, so an atmosphere of admiration is likely to implant a sense of worth in the first place, and to repair one that has been damaged by events.

In addition to these general requirements, children need four things from their parents: love, functionaries, security and knowledge. We shall go on to discuss these in turn, always bearing in mind the underlying aim of offering admiration and stimulation to the children—and remembering, too, that children are all different, so that needs have to be defined and thought out in terms of each individual child.

1 Love

The question of love involves perhaps more misunderstanding and misgivings than any other aspect of stepparenting. Children need love. Without it they fail to develop, or develop all manner of psychological problems that dog them throughout their lives. So much is common knowledge. What is much less clear, however, is what on earth is meant by love and, consequently, what stepparents mean when they say—as they often do—that they do not love their step-children, or not in the same way as they love their 'own' children.

What is clearly not at issue is simply a feeling of tenderness, though obviously it is nice to experience this feeling, which is one of the main rewards of parenthood. Children may from time to time evoke that sort of feeling, and when it occurs we are liable to identify it as love. But such a feeling is not present, day-in-day-out, throughout a child's life. I doubt if anyone could feel tenderness at some

GETTING THROUGH THE DAY 59

aspects of children's behaviour. Nor would such a feeling
be recognisable as love if it involved nothing else. A smelly
baby in a nappy may, or may not, induce a feeling of
tenderness, but love clearly includes changing the nappy. A
toddler may smile charmingly while committing some
outrage and, for all that the smile causes a pulse of
unmistakable affection, love may also require you to stop
the outrage—at the cost of the smile. If you do not stop the
child, it may be injured, or there may be other reasons why
it is not in its interests to carry on with what it is doing. In
such a case, love requires us to sacrifice the feelings of
tenderness in the interests of a less attractive but thought-
out commitment to the child's development. Love involves
caring, in other words, as much as a feeling, and caring is a
matter of effort and commitment, of deliberately planned
routines rather than impulsive emotional expressions.

A feeling of tenderness triggers off an expression of
warmth that is welcome to the child, and this is another
important part of what we mean by love. Once again,
though, such warmth is not likely to be an unvarying
aspect of the relationship between parent and child, but
will come and go according to circumstances. And again it is
not an adequate substitute for the consistent care that is as
much an expression of love as the periodic upsurge of
warmth.

Ideally, then, love will comprise care, tenderness and
warmth, but throughout this book I am arguing against
becoming too preoccupied with the ideal, and arguing for
the wisdom of concentrating on what can be attained with
the resources that are available. A relationship between an
adult and a child should ideally be full of warmth, but many
of them are not, and a relationship that involved nothing
but warmth would not be a lot of use to a developing child.
Nor does the absence of warmth mean that the relationship
is a cold one, if by coldness we mean indifference, for the
caring that is the principal vehicle of love can operate
without much warmth, but be the opposite of indifferent
because of the commitment and thought with which it is
carried out.

Of course I am not advocating the sort of routine, for-

60   STEP-PARENTS AND THEIR CHILDREN

mal caring that a child might have got in a Victorian orphanage. The passionless regime that serves to keep a child fed and sheltered but ignores its emotional needs is certainly not an adequate environment for a child to grow up in (though even then there can be a measure of warmth and tenderness available from the other children which is not to be dismissed). But where warmth and tenderness are not spontaneously present, it does not mean that the care of a child needs to be of that minimal sort. Such care can be augmented by making time for the child, so that it feels wanted; by physical contact where this is appropriate (by which I mean where it will not embarrass the child and there is no possible suggestion of sexuality); by taking extra trouble over routine aspects of care. All these are merely suggestions of how the basic task of caring can be fleshed out by a commitment that can lead to a version of love that is no doubt less rewarding than more spontaneous forms, but can nevertheless go a long way towards meeting a child's need for love.

Before leaving the topic of love (which is touched on in other places in this book), there are two points that need making. The first is that the step-parent is not the only person from whom love is available. The domestic parent, as well as the absent biological parent, is able to provide the love, in all the senses of the word, that a child needs. The task of the step-parent is to ensure that the children get as much as possible of the love available from such sources. This means doing what can be done to prevent the step-parent's demands on the love and attention from the children's biological parent being so insistent that the biological parent has nothing left for the children. Sharing affection in this way is perhaps the hardest part of being a step-parent, and is a principal source of the jealousy that besets step-families (there is a fuller discussion of jealousy and how it can be managed, and to some extent prevented, in Chapter 5). There may also be grandparents, who tradition-ally are able to indulge the warm and tender aspects of love without having to bother too much about its disciplinary and practical aspects. There are other children available as a source of love—not necessarily brothers and sisters, but friends who become increasingly important to children as they grow older. There are domestic animals. For some children there is God. There are the people of a child's imagination. In other words, a step-parent should not be too depressed because his or her version of love is not able to rise above the routine aspects of caring, however conscientiously these are carried out, for the other aspects of love may well be available in other areas of a child's life.

The second point relates to one that I made in Chapter 1. It is very easy for people who are not completely confident in what they are doing to set absurdly high standards by comparing their own performance with that of some imaginary ideal. In practice most families do not lead the lives of orderly affection that they perhaps should do. Many biological parents have pretty mixed feelings about their children for much of the time. Resentment towards their children is as common a reaction as tenderness for many parents. They do things for their children not because they want to, in the sense of getting any particular emotional pleasure out of it, but because they have entered into certain commitments towards their children. There is a routine quality about much, perhaps most, child care that may be lightened by warmth and tenderness, but is not dependent on them. So step-parents who find that they have to make an effort to provide care for their step-children should not underrate the importance of what they are doing, nor devalue it by comparison with some unreal image of 'real' family life.

2   Functionaries

Parents of young children will be aware of a design fault that has left human beings with only two hands. The endless fetching and carrying that children need is the most time-consuming and on the whole least interesting part of bringing them up. The sheer time, to say nothing of the monotony, involved may come as a considerable shock to step-parents who have no children of their own—and they are likely to find themselves resenting it. Most parents will periodically rebel against the diverse jobs they are expected to do—cook, waiter, chauffeur, teacher,

62 STEP-PARENTS AND THEIR CHILDREN

nursemaid, priest, doctor, masseur, butler, salvage expert, and anything else you can think of. The children will listen politely to the mutinous outburst by their adult, and the parent will then knuckle down to it and resume the servitude that parenthood requires. Step-parents, less accustomed to the role, may be less inclined to accept this servitude, but though there is undoubtedly an effort involved, there are a number of reasons why step-parents should not underestimate the importance of the mundane aspects of looking after children.

The first is that these mundane activities provide a tangible way to express care for a child, who almost certainly does not want its parent or step-parent to tell it all the time that the parent loves it—though being told it from time to time is a different matter. What children of all ages want is tangible evidence of love. Getting involved in all the endless administrative aspects of child-care, provided it is done with tact, shows that you wish to become involved in a child's life, that you care enough to spend time on the child, and that you are committing yourself to being involved in the children's daily lives. You may never feel tenderness for your step-children, but by being prepared to give your time, you will be expressing that you value the child, and you are also carrying out a crucial part of parenting; the endless tasks that are essential for the child's social development as well as its physical survival and emotional wellbeing. So, no matter how tedious some of these tasks are, they have a symbolic importance that makes them worthwhile.

Fetching and carrying also provide a useful means of getting involved with the children. A step-parent coming into an existing household does not, of course, usually fetch up on the doorstep as a total stranger to the children with whom he or she is to make a life, but the process of becoming fully integrated into the household is bound to be a slow one, if it ever happens, because the existing household members are usually engaged in patterns of existence that have been worked out to suit their circumstances, and they are probably not minded to change everything to involve a newcomer. But by becoming gradually

GETTING THROUGH THE DAY 63

involved in the practical details of the household's life—perhaps by picking up the children from school, or driving teenagers to a party—the incoming step-parent can often find a space. More importantly, a step-parent can find a way of communicating with the children through doing practical things with them, since settling down for an intimate conversation with a child is usually unrewarding. Such conversations are prone to long and embarrassing silences, and may well leave the child with the impression that you ought to be in some kind of home. But talking about neutral topics while driving a teenager to a party, or while walking home from school, offers children the chance to get to know you, and to develop a relationship that is built around their daily routine, rather than based on a series of intense but unreal conversations. Doing things with people is a better way of getting to know them than interrogating them about their interests and feelings.

Similarly, the household's schedule of chores is the best place for a step-parent to negotiate a place in the life of the family. A single parent is unlikely to be good at all the aspects of parenting and will not have had time or the energy to do everything the children expect. There is, in other words, a vacancy. If the step-parent can take on some of the tasks that the single parent could not do, or never got round to, his or her presence in the household may quickly become intelligible and acceptable to the children, and allow him or her to become increasingly involved in the family's life. Obviously it is important not to get into competition, real or perceived, with any absent biological parent, so tact will be needed to make sure that the step-parent does not appear to the children to be trying to cut out the absent biological parent from their lives. This matter of possible competition with the absent parent is discussed in a little more detail in Chapter 3, and step-parents need to accept that there are limits placed on their activities in the household by the existence of their predecessor. But despite this, the unglamorous business of looking after children's daily needs offers a good starting place from which to develop other aspects of your relationship with them.

64   STEP-PARENTS AND THEIR CHILDREN

3 Security

Children, like all human beings, need security, and it is
important that step-children's sense of security should
not be taken for granted. They will inevitably have
experienced disruptions that will have made them question,
if they have not completely shattered, the structure
in which they live their lives. Some will have experienced a
long period of parental strife before their first household
disintegrated; some will have enjoyed a long and settled
calm with a single-parent household which is then disrupted by the arrival of a step-parent. Whatever the
details, and whatever the age of the children, step-children
will not have had the benefit of the sort of uneventful life
that is supposed to be the rule in conventional families, and
will not therefore have the same basis for security that
children from unbroken homes start with.

It would be a mistake to see step-children as *necessarily*
suffering from a severe level of insecurity. It may be that
their experiences have actually left them feeling more
secure, confident in their ability to adapt to new situations,
and feeling more cared for because their parents had their
welfare as the priority when making the arrangements to
split the household. But more probably step-children will
at best feel unsettled when their step-parent arrives, at
worst completely bewildered. In any event, it makes sense
to assume that a measure of insecurity exists, and that this
needs to be tackled in a systematic way.

If children feel insecure they are liable to behave badly.
This bad behaviour may be unruliness, as they enact the
lack of structure in a chaotic drama. They may behave in
ways that serve to test the structure that they feel
uncertain about—perhaps by doing things to see if the
threatened retaliation really happens or, conversely, by
being scared to do anything because they do not know
what might happen. They may become emotionally withdrawn, afraid to risk emotional expression because they
are unsure how it will be received, or they may become
hysterical in their search for some stable point in their
emotional lives. But however diverse the ways in which a lack
of security may be expressed, it is clear that it will have a

GETTING THROUGH THE DAY 65

severe long-term effect on a child's emotional development, and on an adult's ability to enter satisfying relationships. But though everyone knows that children—and adults—need security, what exactly is it? And, more importantly, since the word itself is not likely to need much explaining, how can we provide it for children? If we attempt to dismantle the idea into a serviceable form, there are a number of aspects that can be suggested as the basis for practical routines. But before doing that, it is worth commenting on a few of the things that security is not. It is not an absence of danger. Obviously we try to protect children as far as possible from danger, physical and emotional, but we know that there are limits on what we can and should do. In terms of physical danger, there comes a point when a parent can do no more, and if a young person wants to take up sky-diving or Russian Roulette, there is nothing much that the parent can do to stop it. But before that point comes, parents will do all that they can to restrain their children's wilder risks, and to steer the narrow course between overprotectiveness and conniving at suicide. Emotionally, however, the idea of danger may be much less easy to make sense of. Parents who watch the heartbreak as a first passionate school friendship falls apart, betrayed by the faithlessness of a five-year-old who has found a new friend, will know that such heartbreak is a necessary part of learning to be human, and that only by risking such pain can important relationships ever develop. But that does not make it any less painful to watch, and we wish that it could be avoided. So security does not mean trying to protect a child from such experiences, but rather creating an atmosphere in which the emotional risks that have to be taken will do the least damage if they go wrong. In other words, there is an important difference between security and smothering, and when we acknowledge that we cannot protect our children from all the chances of life, and it would not be in their interests if we could, we have made a start in defining security in practical ways.

One component of security is routine. On the whole, the lives of children and young people have enough variety and

66 STEP-PARENTS AND THEIR CHILDREN

challenge to make a measure of domestic routine desirable, and they often need a high level of organisation in their lives to manage the tight schedules that their many demands require. Because of this, a routine that is right for the children may involve high costs for the adults in terms of time and convenience, and this may be something that step-parents find makes them especially resentful. But such costs to adults are another price of caring for children, a demonstration of love, and hence important as much because of this as because of the contribution that a routine makes to children's sense of security.

The problem with routine is that it is not exciting. The lack of routine may lead to havoc, as children's and adults' anxiety is expressed in excitable behaviour or testing of the situation, but a routine established at much inconvenience to the adults may earn little thanks. It will probably only be vaguely appreciated by the children on whose behalf the adults have put themselves to so much trouble to provide a settled framework for their lives. Younger children are unaware of the effort that they involve, teenagers take it for granted (if, that is, by any chance they dimly realise it). This being so, the importance for step-parents of the routine may be as a demonstration to themselves that they are prepared to go to a lot of trouble for the children. Doing what someone else needs you to do, rather than what you might prefer to be doing, is the sort of unselfishness that step-parents may need to draw their own attention to from time to time.

Step-children have inevitably experienced some disruption to their lives—and their routines—as the biological home has been replaced by the remade home, and as the step-parent comes on the scene. They may, therefore, need a firm routine more than children who have led less eventful lives, but they may also be suspicious of a new regime that is introduced by a newcomer to their lives, so care and tact are needed in putting a routine into practice. Stability is not an end in itself, and it needs to be firmly anchored in the familiar components of the children's existing routines rather than started afresh. This can be difficult when both adults bring children to the new household, particularly when one side is moving into the house that is already the other side's home. When families are amalgamating in this way, the ideal would be to choose a new home to fit the new household's requirements, but the cost and the availability of suitable housing often rule that out. The best that can be hoped for in such a case is to handle the amalgamation with the maximum respect for existing routines, trying to establish for each child what are the most important aspects of its daily life, and to work out which parts of its routine are most dispensible in terms of the likely effects of losing them.

Security also involves safe boundaries. Children who are brought up without any limitations will be spoiled brats not only because they will seek to get their way by tantrums and other unpleasantness, but because they will never have learned how to negotiate their social situation. If a child has never had any clear limits on what it can and cannot do, and more importantly what it may be able to get away with, it will enter adult life without the experience to make the sort of negotiated deals that social life requires. So orderly domestic life needs clearly-understood rules—which will, of course, change with age—because they form the basis of a person's eventual social skill. I do not think that a rule book is a good idea—and I am quite sure that children who are allowed to behave as they like are on the whole much better equipped for adult life, and much happier, than children whose lives are tyrannically governed by the rules laid down by powerful parents. Somewhere between complete licence and complete control is the ideal; children need to learn how to live socially, and this involves a clear understanding of the rules that govern social life, which means experience of a domestic world in which the ground rules are intelligible. This is what safe boundaries involve.

This introduces the vexed issue of punishment—of which there is a fuller discussion in Chapter 4. If the object of security in the domestic regime is to make children feel safe, and to teach them the basis for civilised social behaviour, then sooner or later adults are going to find themselves in the position of carrying out some threat, or

68 STEP-PARENTS AND THEIR CHILDREN

all these objectives will be put in peril. This is because children who are testing the boundaries of their world and then find that their parents either do not mean what they say or apparently do not consider it worth taking the trouble to do what they say, are liable to be left both insecure and belittled. They will be insecure because certain benchmarks that have been insistently laid down have disappeared, leaving confusion about acceptable behaviour and about the adults' competence, and belittled because the child is apparently not worth the punishing. I am not suggesting that it is possible to destroy the whole structure of a child's security by a single mismanaged incident of having your bluff called, but for step-parents and their partners who are concerned to establish a secure environment for the children, it is important to remember that the children may already have had their basic sense of security seriously undermined by the events that they have lived through, and that consequently they are more prone to be unsettled by ambiguities within the new household. The whole question of punishment is difficult enough in biological families, notoriously complex in step-families; the golden principle is not to get pushed into a corner by threatening something unless you really are prepared to carry it out. This in turn suggests that any threatened sanctions should be pretty mild, and that the household regime should be based on approval and encouragement rather than disapproval and threats. If such a regime has been evolved and accepted as important by a child, then the withdrawal of approval is a clear enough sanction that does not involve dramatic confrontation. But, as I mention in Chapter 4, it is very much easier to talk about punishment than to develop a sensible and effective regime.

To sum up this section, security is something that children need for healthy development. It lowers anxiety, and provides the basis for their negotiation of their own adult social worlds. It can be provided within step-households where the adults recognise its importance, behave in ways that are intended to foster it, and take into account the probability that step-children may as a breed be less basically secure than children of biological households.

4 Knowledge

Parents have an obvious role as teachers. Much of this teaching concerns specific skills—teaching a child to read, to swim, to ride a bike and so on. This sort of teaching is an aspect of parenting in which a step-parent can demonstrate care, and in which a child's trust can be earned, and there is no reason why a step-parent should not perform it as well as a biological parent—with the important proviso that some of these skills are learned only from someone whom the child trusts; so a step-parent should not rush into getting involved before a child is ready. Alongside this training in skill which, as the child grows older, is increasingly carried out by people outside the family, is a more nebulous, but just as important, form of learning—what we may call the rules of the game.

Children learn the ways of the world from a number of sources, most importantly, perhaps, from the social experiences of school; but they pick up values, patterns of personal relationships and an understanding of the ways of the world from their domestic experiences. Often the domestic and the public lessons will be in conflict, leaving the child to work out for itself its own system of beliefs and values, but though it may ultimately reject the instruction in the rules of the game that it has had from home, the importance of this instruction remains.

The instruction is more from demonstration and example than straight precept. This means that when, as in most households, there is some discrepancy between what is practised and what is preached, children are going to be as much impressed by the practice as by the preaching. If adults lecture their children about the importance of honesty, but make no attempt to hide their own shady business dealings, then a child will be confused. Most children are in practice well able to cope with such contradictions, for the rules of the game in this case probably involve hypocrisy, but a step-child may be muddled by the sort of contradiction that may be taken for granted, or not noticed, by another child who has lived with its parents all its life. A step-parent wishing to take seriously the important family task of teaching the

70 STEP-PARENTS AND THEIR CHILDREN

children will do well to bear in mind that the step-parent's version of the rules of the game will lack the authority that comes from familiarity. The child may be sceptical of this new interpretation of how things are in the world, and of how one should best behave, because it is not the interpretation of a well-trusted adult whose wisdom was first recognised when the child was tiny. Some step-parents find this scepticism on the part of their step-children deeply frustrating, as the children ignore the wisdom and understanding of life that has been laboriously put together over many years. Such scepticism is a common feature of adolescence, so this frustration is a common experience of all parents, but in step-families it perhaps starts earlier.

It is, though, in the area of personal relationships that a child has the most to learn from the home, and in this aspect, too, it learns as much from observing as from what is said. In this type of learning, step-children may well be lucky, for there will be aspects of the adults' lives that will be different in step-families, and which may teach step-children useful lessons that children in biological families have less opportunity to learn. In a step-family there is, for instance, often more overt affection between the adults, who may be trying to pack a period of courtship, followed by a honeymoon, into the gaps of caring for children, and it is a good thing for children to see the emotional pleasure of adults (provided, obviously, that it is handled with tact, so that the children are neither embarrassed nor excluded). Similarly, getting to know a new adult in the shape of a step-parent is not something that children in biological households are able to do so well, and again, this is a useful experience in learning about life. The whole delicate area of handling a split household, keeping alive a relationship with a biological parent who has left home and at the same time negotiating a way of life with that parent's successor, may not in itself be a desirable experience, but it can be useful in terms of learning about adults and their relation-ships. So step-children have particular opportunities to learn about personal relationships, that can be a most useful basis for later life.

GETTING THROUGH THE DAY 71

Closely involved in learning is the place of models for behaviour in the life of a child. Adults contribute to children's education and emotional development by offering a model on which the child can base its approach to the world. It may be that for much of its life a child will copy its adult model, though often, especially in adolescence, it will deliberately and noisily reject it. Both approaches have their difficulties. The child who copies may end up as a clone of its parent, with little individuality of its own, while the child who rejects all that its parents stand for may miss out on some of the useful lessons that might be learned from them, and have an unnecessarily difficult time in consequence. But whatever the problems in the process, the presence of a model is almost invariably important in a child's development, and there is no reason why a step-parent should not be a satisfactory one. Indeed, to return to an earlier point, if a step-parent negotiates the emotional and practical difficulties of the situation with wisdom and tact, the child will have the chance to witness a complete repertoire of social and emotional skills to learn from and to copy—more complete than is available in a single-parent household, and available only in different forms in biological families. If the step-parent is a kind and considerate adult, the children will be able to learn much from such an adult about how to be a human being, and to develop social skills from copying the adult's behaviour.

Summary

In this chapter, I have been trying to show that a child's needs are capable of being met within a step-household. The ways in which this happens will almost certainly be different from how they would be met within a biological home, but if things go well there are ways of meeting needs that can potentially be done better by step-parents, because the different experiences on offer may be valuable to a child. And none of the needs is incapable of being met by a step-parent who is committed to doing it, and is able and prepared to make time and imagination available.

3 GETTING THROUGH THE WEEK

This chapter is about the sort of things that disrupt the daily lives of step-families. Throughout this book I have tried to avoid discussing step-families as if they were nothing more than nests of difficulties, for step-families are potentially happy and successful places in which to bring up children. All households have problems, however, and although those that occur in step-families are not always the same as those of biological families, they share the important similarity that domestic difficulties are best seen as challenges to be met or negotiated rather than symptoms of inevitable discord.

The problems that we shall be considering are insoluble in the sense that they are an inevitable and permanent component of domestic life. Money is an example: step-family finance is prone to be complicated; but there is often no simple solution to the complication, and all that may be possible is to accept the situation and determine not to let it make you too frustrated and angry. But it is possible to develop domestic routines and styles of relationship that keep problems firmly in check, and to minimise any damage that they might do to the children or adults in the household.

1 Money
If there can be said to be such a thing as a typical step-family, one of the things about it will be that its finances are not straightforward. Like biological families, most step-families could use more money, but for step-families the matter is complicated by special factors. It may, for example, be financially wiser not to set up a step-family in the first place, because some Social Security rules may favour a single-parent household, and forming a two-parent household can lose income that is not made up by the economies of running one household instead of two.

GETTING THROUGH THE WEEK 73

When step-parents are working to support their partners' children, there is bound to be an occasional sense of resentment unless the commitment to support the children has been fully thought through and the implications considered and accepted. And there are all the confusions caused by the maintenance payments and other economic hangovers from previous families. Where the payments to (or more usually on behalf of) the children are made regularly and without unpleasantness, and where they are not cancelled out by the step-parent's contributions to the upkeep of children by a previous marriage, then such payments are presumably useful enough. Even when they are as trouble-free as possible, though, they may still cause uneasiness, perhaps by making the step-parent feel less than wholly responsible for the step-children, or by affecting Social Security entitlements. The fact is that, for most of us, money is much more than a simple practical utility: it is intimately tied up with our sense of worth and with our values; so what to one household might be a welcome financial bonus as maintenance payments are made regularly and without trouble, may seem a more mixed blessing to another.

It is not always the case that maintenance payments are painlessly received, however. Since they represent a convenient vehicle for carrying grievances, the biological parent may continue his or her feud with a former partner by failing to pay, or by paying irregularly, or with such conspicuous bad grace that the whole business becomes a nightmare. Some biological parents use a somewhat different tactic of being assertively generous and prompt, which has the effect of making their previous partner feel guilty—with probable consequences for the new relationship. Whatever the details, however, one thing is clear: that maintenance payments often have a flavour to them which is missing from income from other sources. At the very least there is none of the pleasure that most other income brings.

Where a step-parent has financial obligations to children from a previous marriage, it hardly ever seems to happen that they are the same as the incoming maintenance. Even when they are, the arrangement still means that the

74 STEP-PARENTS AND THEIR CHILDREN

domestic finances are fragmented, with some of it ear-marked, and an inevitable sense that some of the money is private rather than communal. Such an arrangement is perfectly manageable provided that a sense of resentment is not allowed to build up, but money is often the component that is used to work out domestic tensions, and it is a common source of domestic power. Where there is a feeling that some of the domestic budget is not even potentially in joint hands, then a sense of resentment can easily slip in and start to affect family relationships.

Where there are maintenance payments coming in, the children of the new marriage will be on a different footing—which, because buying things for people has important symbolic overtones, can lead to a sense of discrimination. If you take two children out to buy shoes, with the step-child's shoes being paid for by a biological parent and your biological child's by you, there will probably be nothing that an outsider could find to comment on, because both children will be well shod at the end of the shopping trip. But for the step-parent the transaction may have a feel of discrimination about it, perhaps a niggling sense that you are not somehow completely in control (though buying shoes for children is such a nerve-racking business that I don't suppose anyone ever feels completely in control). Such feelings are probably not in themselves of much importance, but a lot of similar feelings put together may add up to a tension that can become a problem.

When the outgoing maintenance is greater than the incoming, then resentment and frustration can easily build up. The mirror-image to this is when there is no maintenance for the step-children, leaving the step-parent in the position of supporting someone else's children. If a step-parent entered the relationship knowing full well that he or she would be supporting the step-children, then on the face of it there is no basis for complaint, and many step-parents welcome such a situation, which allows them to feel that the children are more completely 'theirs'. But because of the emotional connotations of money, a note of resentment may creep in, sometimes leading to the

GETTING THROUGH THE WEEK 75

conclusion that all this is somehow the step-child's fault (there is nothing logical about this, but many of our minds work this way). This in turn can lead to a build-up of tension and resentment, creating an unpleasant atmosphere and eroding the quality of domestic life.

Another financial aspect of step-families stems from the insurance payout that may have been received when a biological parent has died. Closely linked is the payout from many occupational pension schemes (though the pension itself usually stops when the beneficiary remarries—a strange discouragement to the pursuit of happiness). On the face of it such a situation can hardly be a bad one to be in: a sizeable nest-egg, the mortgage paid off, an income for the children if not the adult, and a new partner with whom to share one's life. But such a fortunate situation is not without its problems. The step-parent may well feel uncomfortable, perhaps diminished in some way, by having a partner with substantial independent wealth, and may feel slightly ridiculous because of the way that gold-diggers are traditionally viewed. This is basically an issue between the adults in the household, rather than something between step-parent and children, but again it may lead to an undesirable edginess in the domestic atmosphere.

A third category of financial intrusion into the smooth running of the household is the matter of wills. Most people are reluctant to make a will because it is an uncomfortable reminder of their mortality, but for step-families it may be even more important than for biological families, because the complications may be greater if you die without making a will, since step-children's entitlement to a share in their step-parent's estate may not be automatic. But perhaps more important than the possible chaos you may leave behind you is that making a will is a pretty clear set of statements about your sense of obligation and your affections. A will is a letter to posterity. It can settle scores, and cause pain and guilt, just as surely as a suicide note. Making a will forces you to put a price on your relative sense of obligation to your step-children as against other possible beneficiaries. It also forces you to commit yourself to this price in a way that will eventually

76 STEP-PARENTS AND THEIR CHILDREN

become public, and which even now is likely to be seen by your spouse. Obviously the dispositions that people make in their wills are based on complex calculations and are not simple descriptions of how they value their heirs. If you decide to leave everything to your biological children, it may be because the step-children are expecting a fortune from a grandparent, or because the biological child has special needs. Obviously, too, there are external constraints at work: the property of a married couple is not available to be disposed of by just one of them, and the children usually only stand to gain from a will when both parents are dead; as often as not, wills only involve the children when both parents are killed simultaneously. But, regardless of these realities, a will requires thought and requires also that clear decisions are made about an adult's responsibility and relationships to the step-children, and this may be an uncomfortable thing to do.

To sort out these difficulties around money requires more an attitude of mind than decisive action. The problems are for the most part vague and insubstantial: the more solid ones, such as the size of maintenance, are, paradoxically, more straightforward to tackle because they are easier to pin down, and there are professional services available. But feeling uncomfortable because your partner has independent means because of an earlier relationship, or because you are not paying for your step-child's shoes, seems trivial, even silly, when it is spelled out. So the first thing is to take seriously these feelings, and to recognise that they can undermine your relationships within the household. Money, to repeat, carries heavy emotional overtones, and for many men the fact that their wife has more money than they do may be emotionally destructive, striking at the social assumptions of the man as bread-winner. Similarly, when money is leaving the domestic budget to support children from a previous union, logic may rule that this is a legitimate expense, but resentment can stem from the widely held belief that we have obligations to our own children that we do not have to those of other people (a belief that the success of step-families does much to discredit). So the uncomfortable

GETTING THROUGH THE WEEK 77

feelings are not just the outpourings of immature greed, but are rooted deep in the assumptions of our society.

Having acknowledged to oneself that one may have feelings about the household's finances over and above the purely technical ones of making ends meet, it is sensible to discuss them with your partner. As readers may have gathered, I do not take the view that adult relationships should necessarily consist of interminable frank discussions, but because of the unique importance of money in articulating relationships within families, and because money requires at least some rational decisions, these feelings are not something that can sensibly be kept to oneself. This is probably more true the less money there is, because when a family is really hard up there will often be a lot of stress associated with this, and if the stress is made worse by the sort of feelings we have been discussing, then one could be storing up trouble. If your partner is aware of your feelings, and respects them no matter how silly they might objectively appear, then there comes the possibility of arranging the family finances in ways that deal as gently as possible with the feelings. You may not be able to do much about maintenance payments to children of a previous marriage—and many parents would not in any case wish to stop paying—but it might make your partner slightly happier if the payments did not come from your joint bank account, or if you did not ask your partner to drop the payments off at the court each week. If you are in the position of being able to manage without the maintenance from the children's biological parent, then it might be possible to save it on their behalf and to accept the full burden of their support yourself (though this would clearly have to be something that the biological parent found acceptable, and which older children would need to have explained to them).

Sometimes there is more money available for some children in the household than others—perhaps where an absent biological parent or grandparent is willing to pay for expensive school trips or holidays that you cannot afford for the other children. Where there is a significant different in age, it may be possible to get round this by

78 STEP-PARENTS AND THEIR CHILDREN

telling the unlucky ones that they are too young (or too old)—a device that most most of us will have had endlessly worked against us as children, and which is scarcely ever accepted with any semblance of good grace, but which at least has the merit of being a familiar component in children's pictures of the world, a persistent indication of adult unfairness that children mostly learn to live with. When such an expedient is not available, because the children are too similar in age, the least promising way out would be to prevent the lucky ones enjoying their good fortune: that would almost certainly create maximum envy and discord. It would be better to explain what the situation is with minimum fuss to the unlucky ones, get your head down and prepare to weather the storm. It is best to avoid adding dramatic details ('You see, dear, Cinderella's mother feels guilty at leaving her and gives her these generous presents to relieve her own guilt'). In a more perfect world it should be possible to explain to the absent parent how much trouble this generosity has caused, and ask that it should not happen again, but as the generosity probably stems from mixed motives, and the trouble might plausibly be seen as your problem and therefore not necessarily unwelcome to the absent parent, such an eminently reasonable approach might not be too effective.

Money, like a number of other human utilities, is despised only by people who have it to excess. For most people, living in a society that articulates its values mainly through money, it is something that has significance beyond its importance as a means of exchange. In families it is notoriously the site of a lot of trouble, a means of communicating things about the relationships, and controlling the domestic universe. In step-families, prone to have more complicated financial affairs than biological families, it is as well constantly to bear in mind the emotional overtones carried by money, and its significance as a means of communication. The uncertainties and problems associated with money may cause it to be the source of strain beyond what might be logical in terms of strict common sense.

2 Access

When a couple splits up, it is something that two people do mainly for their own peace of mind, though they will usually think that it is probably best for the children, because two contented people living apart are generally considered preferable to two miserable ones living together. Life, however, deplores such amiable solutions to the difficulty that it causes, and the outcome of a split relationship is not usually two happy people putting together the bits of their lives and adopting a forgiving and forgetting goodwill towards their former partner. Usually the snarling and recrimination continue, and often they get worse with the years. People seem unable to ask themselves how much responsibility they may have had for getting involved with such a conspicuously worthless example of humanity as they now perceive their former partner to be. The children inevitably get involved in all this. One of the first major disputes at the time of the break-up is the question of access—how often and in what circumstances are the children to see the parent with whom they are not to live. In step-families, these decisions will have been made when the biological family split up, and the step-parent will inherit an arrangement from the past, but the arrival of a step-parent introduces elements into the problems of access over and above those experienced by single-parent households.

In practice, for a lot of children any dispute about access may be purely academic. Research shows that only a minority of absent parents maintain any long-term and regular contact with the children. Why this should be is not straightforward, since most parents presumably intend to keep in touch when the relationship between the partners finally ends; probably the most common reason is the pain that contact with the children involves, often made worse by a lack of enthusiasm about the whole thing felt by the custodial parent. This is the parent, after all, who has to make most of the arrangements to get the children to see the worthless apology for a human being that they would be so much better off without.

Normally, children will want some contact with their

80 STEP-PARENTS AND THEIR CHILDREN

absent parent: our society sets a lot of store by parent-child relations, and this, combined with the network of affection and loyalties that has built up when the family was intact, ensures that the relationship is usually an important one. The fact that so many absent parents fairly quickly drift out of regular and frequent contact with their children probably says more about the essential strain of such an arrangement than about the quality of the relationship. There may be a high price to the children in terms of the disruption and inconvenience, as they have to choose between their own friends and interests and a regular connection with a parent who is proposing a level and a form of companionship with the children that are unusual in biological families—in which children tend to do less and less with their parents as they grow older. There is a risk that access can become a formal, joyless business, especially where the absent parent has no suitable home for the children to visit, which can mean stilted conversations in parks or restaurants. There are households, of course, where the absent parent is a frequent and welcome visitor, maintaining a relationship with the children without effort and strain, and one that resembles a typical relationship between parent and child in its continuity, its short but frequent interactions, its close tie-up with domestic places and routines, and its conversations about daily life in the real world. Such arrangements are the ideal, though not particularly common, and perhaps involving more effort and good humour to maintain them than may seem apparent to an outsider. The rest of this section is concerned with the less amiable solutions to the problems of access that most people achieve.

For the parents in step-families, there are often two competing motives at work: on the one hand it may be very nice to have a relationship between the children and their absent biological parent that involves getting rid of them from time to time and allowing the step-parent and partner to have some time to themselves, free of parenting chores and responsibility. Against that, though, is the wish to put the past behind one. To do this it is convenient to depict the biological parent as responsible for all that went wrong, and to wish to minimise the influence that such a person could have over the children. It may also be convenient or desirable to try to make the new household look as much like a 'real' family as possible, and in 'real' families the children are not forever disappearing to spend time with other adults. In all these motives the step-parent has a heavy stake, but they have more to do with what the parents want than with what may be best for the children. It is possible to imagine children being shipped off to see a parent whom they would prefer never to see again, simply to give the adults with whom they live a chance to get some peace, but it is even more possible to imagine a situation in which children find it very difficult to keep in touch with a greatly loved parent because of the difficulties created by the adults with whom they live.

There is, then, a question of disentangling your own wishes from the needs and desires of the children. It is wrong to use the children and their access to their biological parent to prosecute your quarrel with that parent. The fact that the step-parent and the custodial parent would prefer that the children should not see their absent parent—for whatever reason—does not mean that your preferences should be translated into discouraging children from doing something that they may wish to do. It may genuinely be better to allow the relationship to peter out if the regular meetings are unpleasant or boring to the children, and if they are done as a chore by the parent, but such a decision crawls with problems—for example, the children might well become confused and guilty if they were encouraged to drift into severing such an important relationship. If the hope is that the children will forget the biological parent and simply transfer their allegiance to the step-parent, then discouraging access to the absent parent would be a confidence trick, morally shoddy and hardly likely to have the desired effect when the child realises what is happening.

In all this, the step-parent may be rather on the sidelines in a matter that seems primarily to concern the biological parent and the children, and which probably existed before the step-parent came on the scene. The life of the step-

82 STEP-PARENTS AND THEIR CHILDREN

family, however, may be affected in a number of ways. There is, obviously, a consequence for the whole household if the children are put under emotional pressure and strain by the access to their other parent, and the household is liable to be churned up unless the whole business is managed with restraint and tact. Even if you are determined not to allow the whole business to become the last skirmishing ground of dissolved relationships, there are a number of problems, practical and emotional, that can put this resolve at risk. The practical problems concern travel, money, making arrangement with, and perhaps having to meet, someone that the custodial parent might prefer never to see again. For the most part these practical matters will be irksome rather than seriously difficult, but they are liable to seem more important because of the emotional freight that goes with them. If the practical details of a child's access to its absent parent seem excessively inconvenient or expensive, it is worth asking yourself whether the difficulties are not as much to do with your own resentment and reluctance as with the reality of the issues.

Emotionally, the children may find themselves torn in their loyalties and affection—the more so if they are interrogated by each parent about the other: 'What sort of flat has he got?' 'What's her new man like?' and so on. The trouble here is that natural curiosity on the part of a parent about his or her former partner may be interpreted as hostile questioning by a child, whose best strategy may be to see the lives of each parent as separate entities, distinct areas of its experience, like home and school. Where one parent wants to know about the other's life, there may develop a sense of invaded privacy, and a feeling that there is an inappropriate encroachment from one area of life into the other. The opposite of this is likely to be just as difficult for a child to deal with, and that is the feeling that its life in one parent's home must never be mentioned in the other. So coming home from a day out with the absent parent, a child may not feel that it can talk to its other parent and its step-parent about what has been happening, and this may cost much of the pleasure of the day, and in turn vest the relationship

GETTING THROUGH THE WEEK 83

with the absent parent with secretiveness and a loss of spontaneity. It could also leave a child painfully lonely. There may, for example, come a fateful day when it goes to meet its biological parent and finds a nervous stranger waiting there as well. The possibility of further disruption to its life from the absent parent becoming involved with another potential step-parent could be terrifying to a child, and it would be unfair to leave it with no one to discuss its fears with, simply because a previous partner is no longer mentionable at home.

As well as the effect on everyone in the household of these sorts of pressures on the children, it is as well to recognise the feelings of insecurity and competitiveness that can build up in a step-household as a consequence of the children's relationship with their absent parent. At the most simple level, the non-custodial parent is often in a very easy situation compared with the adults who care full-time for the children, and this can cause resentment. Without having to do the work of child care and the daily grind of dealing with the needs of diverse individuals, absent parents are required only to lay on entertainment for brief periods of the week, and are then free to get on with their lives for the rest of the time. The children may come to see their visits as dramatic fun, in contrast to the mundane daily existence at home, and the absent parent may have none of the disciplinary or other constraints that rob daily life of so much of its zest. Just as people who fall in love with a place when they are on holiday find it a very different proposition if they go to live there, so children may develop an unrealistically glamorous picture of life with their absent parent, based on brief and exciting events, and may draw comparisons with their daily life that step-parent and biological parent may be acutely aware of, and which may make them feel nervous and insecure, conscious of the unsatisfactory places step-families are supposed to be; they may seem to threaten the very existence of the step-family. In handling these feelings of insecurity, one very misguided strategy would be to become involved in a regime that seeks to rival the access visits in drama and entertainment. It *may* be sensible, when the children's age

84 STEP-PARENTS AND THEIR CHILDREN

seems appropriate, to talk to them about your feelings regarding the absent parent. Some children may understand how their relationship with the absent parent makes you uncomfortable, and how you fear it will undermine your relationship with the children because the other parent might turn the children against you by criticisms, or by giving them such a good time that they might prefer to move home. Most children, however, would find that such an approach put intolerable pressure on them, virtually demanding a statement of loyalty and affection, and implicitly requiring that they choose between their step-family and their absent parent, when they quite rightly want relationships with both.

The adults who are caring full-time for the children may be forgiven for feeling that the absent parent has all the fun while they do all the work. Shipping the children off every week may well be a chore, and it may seem to threaten the domestic peace in a number of ways, some more realistic than others. The important thing is to encourage the children to do what they want by making their visits to the absent parent as trouble-free and undramatic as possible, maintaining the commitment to an arrangement and not jumping enthusiastically on a child's first small sign of reluctance as an excuse for discouraging further visits, nor packing reluctant children off to spend a weekend with their other parent so that one can amuse oneself in their absence. Where access raises, as it often does, these issues of competitiveness between the step-parent and the biological parent, this is a matter between two adults, and the children should not be dragged into it. The whole business of access is productive of strain and uncertainty for the children, requiring a lot of emotional work if they are to negotiate it in ways that they feel easy with, and requiring a lot of work, self-discipline and good humour on the part of the adults involved.

3 Names
Names are important because they are part of our identity. If a child calls its step-mother 'Mymmy', it is saying something about the relationship. The child may have been coerced

GETTING THROUGH THE WEEK 85

into using the term to satisfy the step-parent's sense of what is right and of how she sees the relationship, or it may be a spontaneous expression of how the child sees the relationship. But one thing is certain, the use of the word will not have become part of the child's world as effortlessly as small children say the words 'Mummy' and 'Daddy' while they practise making sounds with their lips and teeth. So because names are important, it is worth giving some thought to them and how they might affect the domestic relationship and what they might express about it.

The only rule about names is to do all that you can to make sure that there are no avoidable misunderstandings. This means being certain that schools and other public agencies know when a child's surname is different from that of its parents, and making sure that people who may need to know are clear about the names involved. With teenage children it is probably worth having a separate entry in the telephone directory if their surname is different from yours, and adults need to reconcile themselves to being called by their step-children's surnames and to taking a relaxed attitude to it, rather than instantly correcting the mistake. Many step-children find their situation a little embarrassing, and one way of smoothing their paths is to eliminate as much misunderstanding as you can (I am assuming in this discussion that readers' names follow a traditional English form of a surname preceded by two or more first names; such a pattern is not used by people of, for instance, Asian origin, so schools in urban areas in much of the industrial world are getting used to handling names that do not follow traditional English forms, and will usually have little difficulty with step-family names).

Having done what you can to avoid misunderstanding, there remain three decisions about names: what the members of the household are to call each other, what surnames are to be used, and how they refer to each other. None is a permanent decision, particularly the first, where usage may change with age, and as the relationship itself changes over the years. Of the three, the choice of surname is probably much the most straightforward. It is nowadays not automatic for step-children to change their

86 STEP-PARENTS AND THEIR CHILDREN

names when a parent remarries, even if the parent does so, and there may be legal difficulties in doing so (these are covered in Chapter 8). Even where there are no such problems, the matter needs thought. As more and more women are keeping their 'maiden' names on marriage, it makes sense to think before changing a mother's surname on remarriage. By changing her name, she may wish to make a statement about her relationship with her new husband, or to acknowledge the convention, but it might cause her children less social difficulty if she kept the same name as they have. For the children to change their names symbolises a split from their biological parent that they may not wish to make, or which it would pain them to acknowledge. It might seem an attack on their identity, which is closely tied up with what people call themselves. Occasionally there will be good reasons for changing surnames—the children may wish it, for example, or there may be unfortunate associations carried by the original name—but when it has been decided to change names, the usual caution is required with initials. If you are called Matthews, for example, your step-son will not live to be grateful for your surname if his first names are Brian Uriah. In such a case it might be better to choose a name that everyone in the household likes and for everyone to change.

What the members of the household call each other is a more difficult, and more important, question. Since step-children do not on the whole meet their new adult for the first time on the wedding day, and since they will almost invariably have some sort of relationship with a potential step-parent before the step-parent moves in, or before a formal decision is made to amalgamate households, then the forms of address will already have been negotiated. To call someone 'Mother' or 'Father' is to imply something fairly unmistakable about the relationship. Many step-children, especially younger ones, adopt such terms more or less spontaneously, perhaps when talking to their friends about something that has happened at home, 'The man who lives with my mother' is not the sort of language that most school-aged children use when making arrangements to go swimming with their friends; they are far more likely to say 'My father', for convenience. The more they use the term, the more convenient it will become, and the more they are likely to assume a parental relationship. When something happens like this, the sensible thing might be to accept it. I argued in Chapter 1 that it is not always sensible for the relationship to be made too much like a biological parental one, because that would be to mask important and valuable features about step-families, and because it could imply something untruthful about the relationship. It should never be allowed to happen that children are encouraged to see their step-parents as their 'real' parents if this involves denying the existence or importance of the biological parents. But though it is important that children should know they have another parent—or have had one—it is possible to be too rigid, and to refuse the children the right to define relationships in terms that they wish and which they understand because of a (very proper) wish not to imply something untruthful in the household. So where children start addressing their step-parents as 'Mummy' or 'Daddy', then it is probably best to accept it.

Where there is no such spontaneous use of names, though, the matter requires more thought. It may be nice for a step-parent to be called 'Mother' or 'Father', or it may be the last thing he or she might want, but the step-parents' wishes are only part, and perhaps a minor part of the question. Much more important are the children, and for them to be invited to call someone about whom they probably have mixed feelings by a parental title may be to define a relationship for them in ways that they perhaps do not yet accept, or are unhappy with, or which seem an invitation to repudiate their biological parent. For a small child with the prospect of ten or fifteen years of living with a step-parent, the question of what to call that person is rather different from the case of a teenager who may be expecting to leave home within a couple of years. A very small child who acquires a step-parent before it can talk will quite likely use parental terms, though here the problem may arise later when the child will have to have its situation explained, and somehow make sense of the

88   STEP-PARENTS AND THEIR CHILDREN

reality that this long-established parental figure is not in the same relationship to it as its other adult, nor in the same relationship as the one in which most of its friends live with their parents.

For a child to slip easily into using parental terms to its step-parent may be convenient and appropriate to the adults with whom it is living, but can lead to problems for the absent parent, and for the children's relationship with him or her. To hear one's own children referring to someone else as their parent is not only painful in itself, it is liable to have repercussions. Keeping in touch with the children from a failed marriage is usually an effort, and one that requires a major commitment—and, as we have seen, many absent parents gradually drift out of significant contact with their children. It is hardly much of an encouragement to that effort to hear yourself insensibly replaced in your children's vocabulary by their step-parent, and being written out of their script in favour of someone else.

Any decisions that are reached about names are probably much less important than the fact that people have thought about the question. Thought implies care and an awareness of the possible feelings involved, and this is likely to be a much more significant factor in determining a step-family's happiness than what everybody in the household calls each other. Where the children are old enough, or when they reach an age when they are able to participate, a discussion with them will be an excellent way of showing an adult's concern for their feelings, and will provide a valuable means of exploring family relationships by concentrating on a topic that is important but not too intense. A child's reluctance to call its step-parent 'Mother' or 'Father' will be apparent, even where it is agreed, and may give an important clue to its real feelings about the step-parent—something that it is important for step-parents to understand and accept, even when it is not what the step-parents want to hear.

The third decision about names is how members of the step-household should refer to each other. Many step-parents hate the word 'step', so perhaps the only way to get rid of the unpleasant overtones that the term carries is to

GETTING THROUGH THE WEEK   89

use it with pride, as signifying a worthwhile relationship in which someone has accepted a responsibility for a large share of the care of another human being. Maybe it is, but as with all campaigns, the flag-waving of the parents will no doubt embarrass the children who, as a rule, prefer a measure of anonymity on the part of their adults. So although it might suit the adults' programme to turn up at school and ask 'Is my step-son ready yet?', it might not suit the child to have its relationships made so public, and to have it announced to his friends that it lives in the sort of relationship that every toddler knows to be a difficult and sinister one. Better, perhaps, to ask for the child by name, without defining your relationship, and to spell out the nature of that relationship only when necessary. The situation may change, and step-children could possibly end up as a majority; if this should happen, then the public acknowledgement of the relationship will become common-place. Until that time, a low-key discretion may suit the children best—though this, like everything else, is capable of being negotiated with the children.

4 Grandparents

Becoming a grandparent is supposed to be entirely pleasur-able, involving all the fun of having children and none of the drawbacks. Grandparents traditionally are able to 'spoil' their grandchildren without having to worry about discipline, and to enjoy their company in short bursts without all the work involved in being a parent. It is therefore particularly devastating for many grandparents when their children's marriage ends, and their relationship with the children is liable to feel even more threatened if their grandchildren are absorbed into someone else's home. With the best will in the world, most people are going to find it hard not to take the side of their own child when a marriage has ended in acrimony. This is likely to lead to a measure of reserve in dealing with the in-law, and if the children are living with a son-in-law or daughter-in-law, rather than with one's 'own' child, then it requires a lot of tact and consideration on the part of the in-law to maintain an easy relationship between the children and

90 STEP-PARENTS AND THEIR CHILDREN

their grandparents. Many grandparents are, for obvious reasons, going to feel inhibited about staying in a household when their own child is no longer there.

A child's relationship with its grandparents is often very important, and for a child to lose its grandparents when it loses a parent could be unbearably painful. For children in step-families, whose lives have inevitably seen many changes and who will often feel insecure as a result, the relationship with grandparents may be an essential island of stability in a shifting world. It is therefore important for a child's parents to do all that they can to foster such relationships—and if it happens that you regard your parents-in-law as malevolent busybodies who did much to sabotage your marriage, this is a feeling that should not be allowed to interfere in what is best for the child. For grandparents, it is important to recognise that their wish to see the children is not just for their own benefit, but is probably very important for the child— important enough for grandparents to decide that they may need to overcome an understandable hesitation, and make some moves to keep the relationship alive. There would be an element of betrayal of the child involved, if its relationship with its grandparents were allowed to fizzle out because of diffidence or embarrassment on the part of the grandparents, or because the step-parent has more immediate concerns.

All this becomes even harder when the in-law remarries, and the children become part of a new household. Where the children are old enough, and where the grandparents feel they can manage, the easiest way round this is for the children to visit their grandparents, and for the relationship to be maintained outside the children's household. Where the children are too small for that to be possible, the grandparents may be able to keep in touch with them through their own son or daughter, and to see them at his or her home. Often, though, distance will not allow brief visits, and the children may not be old enough to make longer visits. In this case, the only way in which contact can be maintained will be by the grandparents staying in the step-household. Such a visit is likely to be a daunting prospect, and the responsibility is on the adults in the step-household to make people welcome, and to recognise—without, however, making matters worse by constantly drawing attention to it—how difficult such a visit is and, at an elementary but practical level, making sure that such visits take place when the children are around to see their grandparents—in school holidays, for example.

In many cases, when a marriage breaks down, the grandparents become more deeply involved with the children, perhaps taking on some of the activities usually carried out by the missing parent. Grandparents are entitled to have these arrangements honoured by an incoming step-parent. If you have got into the habit of taking your grandchildren to watch football matches because it is traditional in your family for the men to do this with the children, and they have no father available to do it, then it is going to be hard to cede this responsibility to a step-parent when he comes along, and there is no reason why you should, as it would be unpardonably insensitive for a step-father to try to usurp the grandfather's role in this way. It is worth insisting to any grandparents who may read this book, as well as to the adults who have daily charge of the children, that the relationship between a child and its grandparents is worth protecting, and grandparents should not allow themselves to be pushed aside because the relationship is not altogether convenient to the adults in the step-family. This said, it is by no means easy for grandparents to assert their rights, since they may be confused by the strangeness of the situation, they are often on their own, and they have nothing to back their claims. It is usually up to the adults in the step-household, therefore, to make matters as easy as possible for the grandparents.

The second area of conflict for grandparents is their position, and how they should react and behave, when their child acquires step-children, thereby making them step-grandparents. Faced with such an event, most people might reasonably ask how on earth they are supposed to react. There are no rules or guidelines. What should they call these children? What should the children call them?

92 STEP-PARENTS AND THEIR CHILDREN

Should they give them birthday presents? Have them to stay? And behind this kind of questioning lies a second range of uncertainty, about one's feelings about divorce and remarriage, about one's sense of obligation to the children of one's own family as against those of another family. Many people in this situation solve things by keeping well out of the way, having as little as possible to do with their child who has acquired step-children and, while making no conscious decision about how to react to them, in practice virtually ignoring them. At the other extreme are people who 'adopt' the step-grandchildren, treating them identically with their other grandchildren. If one can bring oneself to do it, this second approach has much to be said for it, signalling that step-children are full members of the family—much as would happen, one hopes, if the children were adopted and became family members by that means. Midway between these two approaches would be a compromise, whereby the grand-parents accept the step-children up to a point, but not as completely as the other grandchildren. So, for instance, the step-children get smaller Christmas presents than the other grandchildren, but are treated as people who have some rights, and at least some relationship with the grandparents.

Where favouritism on the part of grandparents gets too obvious, a word with the grandparents may help. As often as not it will stem not from any wish to be unpleasant, but from unconsidered assumptions about what is 'right'—and the assumptions about how one should behave towards one's grandchildren contain no ruling on step-children. The adults caring for the children need a lot of tact, having on the one hand to cope with the moans of the children who are getting the thin end of the wedge of grandparental attention, and on the other recognising that an older generation may have a lot of trouble accepting divorce, and that grandparents may be making a major effort, but be unable to treat their step-grandchildren exactly like their biological grandchildren. To insist on equal treatment may be important in terms of your commitment to all the members of the household, but could be an impossible and cruel demand on a grandparent.

4 DISCIPLINE, REWARDS AND PUNISHMENTS

By 'discipline' I do not mean just punishment and obedience, but all the customs and expectations about behaviour that exist in the household. Such customs and expectations are supported by rewards as well as by punishments—in sensible households very much more—so the whole life of the household is brought together in this use of the term discipline. This chapter, then, is not just about how a step-parent might set about securing 'desirable' behaviour in the household; it is about domestic harmony, and how a regime can be evolved that is not merely an expression of parental authority. Much more is conveyed about relationships and feelings by actions and routines than by words. So if, for instance, you profess overwhelming affection for the children, yet expect them to be in bed before you get home and make a fuss if they are not, then the message of the disciplinary regime is going to be at odds with what you say. Discipline, in other words, needs to reflect the intention to care for the children of the household, and this is rather harder to achieve than simply getting them to jump to it at every instruction.

Even in the sense of discipline that I have described there is an element of authority, although authority means much more than bossiness. The adults in a household have authority because of their age, their experience, their competence, and because the children trust and respect them. Step-parents usually have much less of this natural authority than biological parents, so the question of discipline brings together all the problems of step-parenting. It is difficult enough to manage discipline within biological families—where at least the children have grown up with an assumption that their parents have some sort of right to make the household rules, and to impose sanctions

94 STEP-PARENTS AND THEIR CHILDREN

when they are broken—but step-families have to start from scratch, and to work out from first principles what the domestic regime is to consist of, what standards the children are to be taught, what sort of behaviour is to be expected, and what is to be done if the children fail to comply. This domestic regime has to cope with two overwhelming difficulties. First, it has to compete with what went before—what life was like in the single-parent household that preceded it, and what it was like in the original biological household. When it differs from what went before, as it is almost bound to, it has to secure the children's—and often the biological parent's—recognition that what is now being expected is fair and legitimate. The second difficulty is one that step-families share with biological families, only in a more acute form, and that is finding an acceptable route between the wishes of the parents about behaviour, based on their experience and philosophy of life, and the legitimate needs of children to take increasing responsibility for their own behaviour, and to do what they feel they should, not what their parents want them to, as they develop towards adulthood.

A step-parent can feel under strong pressure to do something about discipline, partly because that is what is expected of the adults in a household, partly because the biological parent may need help with the disciplinary aspects of bringing up the children, and partly because the step-parent's domestic peace requires at least some co-operation from the children. This chapter is an exploration of some of the issues involved in discipline, starting from the insistent point that there are few straightforward principles in what is probably the most difficult and challenging part of parenting. The only two 'rules' that can be relied upon are, first, that the nature of the problem of discipline is decided by the nature of the emotional relationships between the people involved; and, second, because a step-parent is starting from the basis of what went before, since the children have already been living in a disciplinary relationship with their biological parent, the step-parent's best bet is to ease him- or herself into existing arrangements, respecting them as expressions of the

DISCIPLINE, REWARDS AND PUNISHMENTS 95

relationship between the children and the biological parent, and not being tempted into trying any 'new broom' tactics. Bringing up children is everywhere a matter of two steps forward and one back, and this is true in the area of discipline above all.

The matter of discipline is made even more difficult by the likelihood that a step-parent will have got involved in it, and therefore have got embroiled in behaving in certain ways, before he or she has given the matter much thought. A lot of step-parenting is an exercise in retrieving situations, and step-parents will often find themselves trying to wriggle off disciplinary hooks upon which they have impaled themselves, because they have taken for granted things that, with hindsight, seem rather less obvious. You may, for example, have got into the habit of shipping the children off to bed rather earlier than they have been used to, and be doing this for all sorts of sensible reasons, only to find that you are causing resentment that is spilling over into other areas of life, and which would have been avoided if you had thought through the question of bedtime before, not after, it led to trouble. A newcomer to the household is likely enough, as an adult, to make assumptions that his or her wishes should prevail. Insecure and uncertain, a new step-parent is liable to have these feelings made worse if the children ignore what they are told, and an angry power struggle can quickly develop. Almost unawares, everyone finds themselves involved in an escalation of conflict, in which step-parents become increasingly coercive in getting their way, because not getting it makes them feel so inadequate, and the children develop an increasingly mutinous acquiescence based not on a recognition of the step-parent's wisdom and sense, or even on a wish to get the step-parent's approval, but on fear and anger. If the children demur—as most children sometimes will—when asked to do something, the step-parent can become frustrated by the lack of respect. Frustration causes tempers to rise, and a nasty situation may develop, consisting of enraged impotence, often spilling over into violence on one side and sullen resentment on the other. It is a little late to start to think about

96 STEP-PARENTS AND THEIR CHILDREN

discipline when things have reached this pass, though even belatedly clearing one's head about the issues at stake may help to avoid similar pointless confrontations, and to prevent the build-up of resentment that comes from constantly repeated episodes of this sort.

Obviously the answers to all these questions will vary according to the usual variable factors in step-families— the ages of the children, the gender of the step-parent and the children, and how long the step-parent and the children have known each other. Where a step-parent has been on the scene since a child was tiny, then the child will grow up accepting the adult's right to decide the household rules, and any resentment will be more the natural result of restless independence than of a 'who does he think he is?' resentment of a new broom. Younger children in any case are perhaps more prone than teenagers to do what adults tell them, though some children are so habituated to obedience that they show less of a healthy questioning attitude to people giving orders.

Just as the details will vary greatly, so will the emotional arena in which the matter of discipline is played out. Some children will be so used to their step-parents from their experience of them before they joined the household that they will be disposed to comply with their wishes out of affection or respect. Other children will be so worried about the step-parents and anxious to please that they will take aboard their value system—but much as people caught up in terrorist kidnaps sometimes end up accepting their captors' ideologies, as fear turns into an anxiety to please, which in turn translates into sympathy for the cause. In other words, though you may seem to be experiencing no disciplinary problems, it does not follow that there are none: the children could be too cowed to resist, because they are living in a domestic regime of fear and resentment rather than relaxed affection.

I had better make my basic position on all this clear at the outset. I do not believe that instant obedience to every adult command is a healthy thing to inculcate into children. If you want someone to spring to attention at your every whim, you should get a dog. Nor do I believe that adults

DISCIPLINE, REWARDS AND PUNISHMENTS 97

have some special knowledge or wisdom that entitles them to decide the household rules and impose them on children. This is especially true of step-parents. The only right that a step-parent has to decide how children should behave is the one that is earned by gaining their respect, and with it the recognition that the step-parent has enough wisdom and experience to be worth listening to. You may be able to impose your wishes about behaviour on the children because you are an adult, and consequently more powerful (because you are stronger and richer than they are); but being able to do something doesn't mean that you have the right to do it, and imposing your wishes on children who recognise only your power, not your right, is a certain route to disaster. Sooner or later the children will be able to repudiate your authority, and when they do it the accumulated resentment will make the process immeasurably nastier than the inevitably unpleasant time when children finally break free of their parents' control as they achieve self-sufficient adulthood. Adolescent rebellion is not the easiest thing to live with, but it is potentially horrendous where the step-parent has exercised discipline that the children have seen as arbitrary.

In order to pull together all these ideas into some form of practical and harmonious regime for a step-family, there are four broad questions that need to be roughly resolved. The first concerns the purpose of domestic discipline, the second is to decide how significant it might be if the children fail to comply with your wishes, the third is what to do in order to get them to behave as you think they should, and the fourth is the nature of the step-parent's relationship with the children.

1   What is Discipline For?

There are three purposes in domestic discipline. The first is to protect the children from harm—which may be physical, like falling in a pond, or emotional, like making friendships that will lead to pain. The second is to protect the parents. This may be short-term, like stopping the sort of noise that is driving you to screaming point, or it may be long-term, in protecting the adults' morale and self-esteem. The third is

98   STEP-PARENTS AND THEIR CHILDREN

the training of children in the social skills and practices that make for an harmonious life with other people. Let us take these three purposes separately.

Protecting children from harm seems to me the most important point of discipline, though it is less straight-forward than it might seem. It does not mean protecting children from all risks. In all aspects of life, some measure of risk may be necessary if there are to be any rewards. This is particularly true of relationships, where the full richness of experience is only available to people who are prepared to risk being hurt. The possibility of pain is the price that intimacy exacts from its beneficiaries. And a lot of the things that people find most enjoyable entail physical risk, from rock-climbing to riding, fishing to going to work. The point about emotional risks is to try to ensure that when they do not come off the pain is not irreversibly destructive, and that physical risks are taken with a sensible estimate of the odds. The practical applications of all this in terms of caring for children are dependent on age, for with very young children it is first necessary for them to learn that there is such a thing as danger—which most of them seem to do without breaking too many bones, though at a high cost to the peace of mind of their parents. This often involves crude physical constraint—scooping up a child as it hurtles towards an oncoming bus, rather than spending valuable time reasoning with it. Later, as per-manent supervision becomes impracticable, children have to be taught how to cross roads, not to talk to strangers, and the general repertoire of common prudence that is essential to survival. But they are still going to want bicycles, and fireworks, to go to the fair or play football, and no matter how careful one is, all such activities involve some risk. So the protection of children is an aspect of discipline that means doing all that can be done to cut down risk, but incorporating the sense that risk is an essential part of life, not an undesirable one, and that over-protectiveness is a poor preparation for life.

This point needs some labouring, because, as I argued in Chapter 1, many adults in step-families are deeply guilty about all that has happened, having been responsible, at

DISCIPLINE, REWARDS AND PUNISHMENTS 99

least in part, for the break-up of the children's original
home, and having caused further disruption by importing a
step-parent into their lives. Guilt can easily find expression
in over-protectiveness, an exaggerated wish not to allow
the possibility of further harm befalling the luckless
victims of one's own previous lack of care for their
interests. Such an attitude is perfectly understandable, but
can lead to a restricted and dull life for the children who, if
their lives are cramped to assuage their parents' guilt,
become doubly the victims of anything that their parents
may have done.

The second aspect of discipline is concerned with the
parents' image of themselves. If our children take not a
blind bit of notice of what we say, we are liable to feel
ineffective, which is an unpleasant and demoralising
sensation. Much better, surely, to have children whose
respect for us makes them carry out our least wish without
argument or delay. That may be the recipe for a peaceful
life at home. It is also the recipe for a home that the children
will want to leave at the earliest opportunity, and in which
they will never develop the self-discipline that they are
going to need fairly early in their school lives, and
throughout their adult existence. People who have been
brought up to do everything they are told will be passive
adults, feeling permanently insecure when parental control
is missing, and vesting parental authority in army sergeants
or senior people at work.

But though we may know with our heads that a regime
of instant obedience is not a desirable one for the children's
emotional and moral growth, nevertheless its attractions
are obvious—a pla´ d household, in which your wishes are
invariably carried out, and in which your assessments are
always accepted. Since we only make decisions that we
believe to be right at the time, it would follow that such a
regime would embody our own wisdom, and would by
definition be in everyone's best interests. 'Mummy/Daddy
knows best, dear,' we are prone to say (and to believe), and
it would be silly to deny that parents do have some claim to
be taken seriously (and obeyed) by their children, if only
because they are older and will have learned at least some

100 STEP-PARENTS AND THEIR CHILDREN

wisdom with the passing years. So when an argumentative or disobedient child flouts this legitimate authority, parents are going to feel that their sense of personal worth and achievement is being challenged, and that the child is behaving self-destructively by not availing itself of the benefit of the adults' experience.

All this is liable to find a focus in the sort of battle of wills that involves a tight-lipped parent saying to any passing stranger who will listen that 'this is one I have to win', as he or she attempts to impose some arbitrary command on a recalcitrant child. Usually common sense prevails, and a compromise is sought which preserves the adult's sense of control, and lets the child off with an approximation of what is required (putting some of its toys away, perhaps, instead of them all . . . well, perhaps one toy . . . well, will you help me put this one away? . . . look, you little swine . . .). But common sense does not always prevail, and a power struggle about something essentially trivial may be pursued to victory—and defeat. Bringing up children is not a war, though it may seem like one occasionally, so there should be no battles, and the language of winning and losing should be entirely irrelevant. But because the self-esteem of adults is tied up in discipline, and because most adults wish children to do things only if they believe them to be in the child's interest, bringing up children often lacks the give and take of civilised debate. Reason and calmness are often crowded out, and an adversarial atmosphere builds up.

I have perhaps painted the aspect of an adult's self-esteem in the matter of discipline in rather harsh colours. The sense of personal value that adults get from being parents is legitimate and pleasant, and is one of the most significant rewards of parenthood. The sense of being accepted by the children is one of the most important and moving rewards that a step-parent can expect. But respect has to be earned, to be allowed to develop spontaneously, not imposed. What is essential is not to allow the matter of domestic discipline to become the vehicle for fostering an adult's sense of importance, nor to allow this to become the litmus test of one's role in the household. Much better to

DISCIPLINE, REWARDS AND PUNISHMENTS **101**

keep out of discipline altogether—or as far as possible—
than to allow it to become a battleground.

The third aspect of discipline is to teach children how to
live as social beings. When a baby is born it has undoubted
charms, but it can only loosely be described as a social
being, if by that we mean an ability to give and take, to
adapt one's own needs to accommodate those of others,
share tasks and responsibilities, and enmesh one's own
wishes with those of other people in an harmonious whole.
Babies are not good at any of this, though they require a
high level of such social capabilities in those who are
caring for them. The slow recognition that one is not the
centre of the universe is not the most pleasant part of
emerging to an adult awareness—and being in love can at
least in part be explained by the mutual discovery of
someone who is prepared to replace you in your rightful
position at the centre of things that you enjoyed as a baby.
And giving up the charms of babyhood in favour of more
co-operative ways of being is a disagreeable piece of
childhood, something that children engage in very reluctantly, with much mutinous backtracking and general
unpleasantness. Persuading a child to help with the
washing up, or tidy its bedroom, or in any minimal way to
behave like a civilised sociable being is, alas, hard work, but
if it is not done, the child may harbour illusions about its
social role and responsibilities that will serve it ill in later
life.

2   Naughtiness, Iniquity and Vice

Always remembering that virtuous behaviour may be just
as ominous as bad behaviour in terms of what it has to say
about relationships within the household, it is usually bad
behaviour that forces some sort of action. It is a depressing
feature of human life that we are mostly concerned much
more about people who do not conform to our expectations
than about those who do. Discipline is usually conceived in
terms of disobedience, not obedience; too few parents
worry about why their children do everything they are
told, and far too many get disproportionately bothered
about trivial delinquencies. Too much obedience could be a

102 STEP-PARENTS AND THEIR CHILDREN

real cause for concern, especially in a step-family, as it might be based on insecurity and fear, which are very unhealthy reasons for any sort of behaviour. If you feel that there are no 'disciplinary problems' in your step-family, you should skip this section, but consider very hard whether your situation is the result of good fortune, good management or tyranny.

Few households are free of behaviour that the adults consider undesirable—and probably even fewer are free of adult behaviour that is entirely to the children's taste. As this is a book aimed primarily at step-parents, we shall abandon democratic concerns and concentrate on why children behave badly. First, though, we need to define bad behaviour in order to keep it in proportion. Much behaviour that adults try to suppress is irritating rather than morally significant—though that does not make it unimportant, for it is the build-up of irritation that sometimes leads to catastrophe, not just major shortcomings of character. It happens, for example, that I, who readers will by now know to be a model of genial humanity, find people who scribble on telephone directories so irritating that I am to be found prowling in the garden shed to see what pesticides might be adapted to deal with them. A member of my household who disfigures my Rembrandts or (more plausibly, since my house lacks Rembrandts) plays with my watch in the bath, has much less to fear than one who carelessly writes the plumber's 'phone number on the telephone directory. In step-families, however, irritating behaviour may be irritating for reasons that are not completely trivial, for some of the underlying tensions within the household may attach to fairly harmless behaviour and give it a quality that a step-parent finds infuriating. If, for example, you find your step-child's incorrigible lateness particularly irritating, it might be that you resent the level of responsibility required of you in the household, when what you would really like is to drift along like your step-child and have your life managed for you by your partner, as the step-child's is. It is worth asking oneself, therefore, why particular behaviour is especially irritating, and whether there are more important tensions

DISCIPLINE, REWARDS AND PUNISHMENTS   103

being brought into play by small pieces of behaviour that are in themselves unimportant (I have to report that I have not been successful in interpreting my own concerns with disfigured telephone directories).

Some 'bad' behaviour is irritating, then, rather than significant—though it may be intentionally and systematically irritating. Other forms of bad behaviour—what we call 'naughty', or more serious terms, like 'criminal' or 'wicked', depending on the culprit's age and our own moral opinions—may or may not have some significance in the life of the household or in terms of society outside the home. Why do children and young people misbehave?

a   *Inexperience*

Much bad behaviour is the result of inexperience; children have not yet learned what is and what is not 'done', and their behaviour annoys adults not because they want to be annoying, but because they have made a genuine mistake. A two-year-old who helpfully crayons all over the new wallpaper that you have spent two days putting up, can hardly be described as naughty, and it would be absurd to punish it unless it was obviously an act of delinquency. Bad behaviour stemming from inexperience is relatively easily handled by explaining to the child why its behaviour is unacceptable, and an important part of parenting is just such instruction in social living—what we called 'the rules of the game' in Chapter 2. There is no reason why a well-established step-parent should not do this aspect of parenting, which mainly needs tolerant common sense to control your anger over the ruined wallpaper.

Other sorts of 'bad' behaviour stem from the inexperience of the adults, who define something as bad or naughty when it is actually normal behaviour for a child of a particular age. We may wish to discourage a five-year-old from playing with its genitals, but we need to be clear that the child's behaviour is not some moral outrage—as it might be in an older child—but something that most children do, and have to learn to do more unobtrusively. In such a case, to start screaming threats about 'chopping it off' is hardly sensible, because it mistakes the reason for

104 STEP-PARENTS AND THEIR CHILDREN

the child's behaviour. A great deal of 'bad' behaviour has to do with adults imposing adult standards where they are inappropriate.

Much unacceptable behaviour, then, is more a feature of a child's age than of its moral stature. Behaviour that is intentionally bad is not uncommon, of course, though I have to say that throughout my adult life I have tended to find that being bad was more fun than being good, so the attractions of naughtiness are fairly self-evident to me. The art lies in not getting caught, and I should be much happier to have a child who was cheerfully and openly naughty than one who had the sort of guile that adults practise. But there are forms of bad behaviour that are more sinister, and need to be taken far more seriously when they occur in step-families. I shall distinguish two forms of behaviour that seem to me to be especially worrying.

b *Getting attention*
There is some behaviour that is worrying as well as inconvenient. One example of this is the sort of behaviour that is intended mainly to get attention. Bad behaviour is an efficient way of getting yourself noticed, and some children find that they can only get attention by bad behaviour that leads to punishment. Adults who are of the 'seen and not heard' brigade may be liable to take no notice of the children when they are quiet and orderly, and to take a disproportionate interest when they are disorderly. If your children can only get your attention by making a nuisance of themselves, then it is time to consider a new regime in the household which allows the children to be noticed without the necessity of being troublesome. It is likely that step-children are more than averagely likely to be troublesome because they want attention. Their closest relationship with an adult has at some stage been upset by the arrival of a newcomer who takes some of the time and attention that once belonged to them. A child who feels neglected and insecure in the new arrangement may easily hit upon the strategy of bad behaviour to recover at least some of the missing attention.

DISCIPLINE, REWARDS AND PUNISHMENTS 105

c *Expressing unhappiness*

To punish a child whose behaviour is mainly an attempt to get noticed is scarcely very sensible. It is even more inappropriate in handling a child whose behaviour is an expression of inner turmoil. As we shall see in Chapter 6, step-children are people whose lives have been greatly affected by loss, and this is liable to leave them angry, or hurt, or guilty, or insecure, or depressed, and often a combination of all of these. A child who is angry—perhaps at the loss of its biological parent—is quite likely to lash out at the world in retaliation; if it is depressed as well—and anger and depression go hand in hand—it may not care what other people think of it. A combination such as this can lead to highly destructive behaviour. Some step-children hold themselves to blame for the break-up of their original family, and may behave in ways that serve to secure punishment for their (imagined) wrongdoing. Some step-children will focus all their distress on their step-parent, who makes a handy scapegoat for everything that is wrong in a child's life, and behave towards the step-parent in punishing or vindictive ways, in retaliation for all the wrongs that they are presumed to have done. A step-child's emotions, in other words, may be dramatised in behaviour that is conventionally seen as bad, but which is better understood as an expression of unhappiness than of moral defiance or moral shortcoming.

It is likely to be painful for a step-parent to have to face that a child is behaving as it is because it is unhappy, and that at least a part of the cause of the unhappiness is the presence of the step-parent. If you have treated a child with kindness, it is scant reward to have your kindness repaid by behaviour that reveals that a child is unhappy despite your efforts. It may be easier for the adults to dismiss such fanciful explanations of the child's behaviour, and take refuge in explanations of naughtiness that do not imply any responsibility on the part of the adults—and, to repeat, some naughtiness is simply cheerful wrongdoing, with no ominous overtones beyond a natural curiosity about what one might be able to get away with. If you decide, after giving the matter careful thought, that you are dealing

106   STEP-PARENTS AND THEIR CHILDREN

with nothing more than childish naughtiness or adolescent rebellion, or some other normal feature of social living, then you may conclude that some form of punishment is appropriate. But if it seems that what you are considering is behaviour that reflects the emotional difficulties of your individual household, especially difficulties associated with the presence of a step-parent, then punishment would probably lead to catastrophe.

3 How to Achieve Discipline: Rewards and Punishments
The adults in a household usually have greater power than the children, and this means that they have some measure of control over the rewards and punishments that are used to bring about the behaviour that is assumed to be needed for the harmonious running of the family, and for the children to develop into socially satisfactory adults. I have already made it clear that adults should exercise this power with much thought and humility, not accept it as a natural right, and that since step-parents in general have less legitimate power than biological parents, they need to be especially careful about trying to get their own wishes carried out by the children. But with this important proviso, that parental power carries with it alarming responsibility, there is little doubt that adults have a great measure of control over the rewards and punishments in a household, and the capacity to use or abuse them, so a major aspect of discipline is using these powers in sensible and responsible ways.

Punishments and rewards are not separate possibilities, but closely tied up together. It is not a simple matter of choosing between them, for the absence of reward can be seen as punishment, the absence of punishment can become a reward. We have a brutal joke in our household: 'Do you know what you will get if you stop making such a noise? You will get to keep your teeth.' This said, though, the merits of concentrating on rewards, and using punishment sparingly or not at all, are clear enough for step-parents. If you ignore 'bad' behaviour, you may be punishing it, because taking no notice of someone is a form of punishment, but you are less likely to do any lasting

DISCIPLINE, REWARDS AND PUNISHMENTS 107

harm than by punishing it in a more active way. The first part of this section, then, is a discussion of punishment, with the clear aim of persuading readers that punishment is an extremely unwise thing for a step-parent to engage in. I shall then turn to the more congenial subject of rewards, and argue that a step-child's moral development is more likely to be enhanced by rewards than by punishment.

There are issues of punishment within step-families over and above the general question of whether, or in what circumstances, one should punish children. It is unlikely that the step-parent's relationship with them will be identical with that of a biological parent, which imparts different connotations to any act of punishment. The children, for example, may take for granted a biological parent's right to punish them, and accept the motives for it, but not be prepared to transfer this right to a step-parent, whose disciplinary endeavours may therefore be bitterly resented. There are also the sort of tensions in step-families that we consider elsewhere in this book—the jealousy, resentment, anger, favouritism, scapegoating. All these are liable to find a place within any punishment that goes on, and at best give an ugly flavour to it, at worst make it dangerous and destructive; for in punishment we are playing with an aspect of human relationships that can lead to hatred, anger, despair and death.

Any proposals to punish step-children, therefore, should be considered in the light of the special nature of step-families, with the likelihood that a punishing step-parent will be viewed in a different light from a punishing biological parent, and that there are special factors at work. Because there are major questions about the wisdom of punishing children, sensible step-parents will do well to give this matter a great deal of thought, and to work out what effect their actions might have on the children and on their relationship with them. There will be circumstances when punishment may be an acceptable function of a step-parent's place in the household—perhaps in those cases where the children can never remember a time when the step-parent was not around, and have become accustomed to see the biological parent and the step-parent in the same

108 STEP-PARENTS AND THEIR CHILDREN

light. In such cases, punishment may be reasonably harmless. As a general rule, however, any punishment that occurs would almost certainly be less damaging if carried out by the biological parent.

One aspect of punishment is important, and that is the exercise in self-justification that can follow from what is actually an undignified loss of control. We may do something to children when we are in a temper, and then try to justify it afterwards as part of some worked out system of moral reform—'knocking some sense into' is a phrase we may use to give an undisciplined outburst some spurious legitimacy. Sometimes children will drive us to lose control, sometimes we lose control because of factors that are not the children's fault—we may be tired, or under stress, for example—but when this has happened, and everyone has calmed down, the most sensible course is to regret what has happened, to resolve to try to behave better in future, and not to delude ourselves that our outburst was anything except a potentially lethal breakdown of our own, not the children's, moral nature. It will probably do far more for everyone concerned to apologise to the children rather than try to justify the unjustifiable.

If there is any truth in the explanations for 'bad' behaviour that we discussed in the last section, it follows that the idea of punishment is usually irrelevant in bringing up children, since for the most part their behaviour is not any serious defiance of authority that can be controlled by punishment, but behaviour that is essentially innocent and best handled by explanation, or caused by emotional problems that are not likely to be improved by sanctions. In general, then, step-families will do much better to rely on rewards rather than punishments to achieve a pleasant domestic world and children who are sociable outside the home. But before turning to the more agreeable matter of rewards, we need to look a little closer at punishment to see whether there are any circumstances in which it might be justified.

It is important to distinguish between formal and informal punishment. Formal punishment is the inflicting of penalties in acknowledged retaliation for some mis-

DISCIPLINE, REWARDS AND PUNISHMENTS 109

demeanour. Informal punishment is not so public, and involves things like sulking and ignoring someone, and it may not be connected in the victim's mind with a specific wrongdoing. Both forms of punishment have their own particular dangers, so we shall discuss them one at a time.

Formal punishment is the linking of sanctions to specific offences, a domestic reflection of the criminal justice system. It is worth commenting that few people involved in the penal system have any confidence that the punishments imposed by courts do much to reform individual offenders or deter others from crime, so households that conduct trials and punish offenders might do well to consider why they need to engage in this sort of activity. The very fact that someone in the household—almost invariably, of course, a child—has done something that merits punishment is an indication that the sanctions operating within the household are not sufficient to stop wrongdoing. In the criminal justice system, the tendency is to go on increasing the penalties, in the somewhat illogical belief that more of something that has not worked must sooner or later do the trick. Within families, when something does not work, that might seem a good time to try something different.

It will be clear by now that I do not think much of formal punishment as a tool in bringing up children. Children learn their morality and behaviour in complex ways, not from a simple system of rewards and punishment, and when parents punish children they should not delude themselves that this is the only, or the best, way to induce some civilised behaviour into juvenile savages. One common motive for punishing children is because exasperated adults make threats and then feel they have to carry them out. They find themselves trapped in an 'if you do that I shall . . .' confrontation and try to resolve the dilemma by action. It could, in theory, leave a child confused and worried if you do not carry out your threat, but provided such confrontations are not a regular feature of your dealings with the children, when they could either become meaningless or damaging to the child's development, then the fact that an adult has got him - or herself spiked on this particular hook is usually more important in terms of adult

110 STEP-PARENTS AND THEIR CHILDREN

foolishness than in terms of a child's long-term welfare. Go
to any supermarket and observe the shoppers, and if you
do not first get arrested as a suspected shoplifter, it will not
be long before you see enacted the familiar litany of a
harassed parent—usually a mother, because women tend
to do the shopping—ordering a child to stop doing
whatever it is doing, or else, and the child going on with
what it is supposed not to be doing, with violent consequences. As what the child is doing is invariably more
irritating than important (if, that is, you take the view that
supermarket managers should set out their goods in ways
that discourage young children from damaging them), then
beating up a child in a supermarket, for all that most of us
are liable to do it, is a public demonstration that punishment
has usually got far more to do with the self-esteem of the
punisher than with any larger questions of moral importance.

If you must punish, then, do not fool yourself that you
are doing the child a favour, and do not assume that an
unpunished child will grow up to be delinquent or
incapable of social living. And if you decide that punishment
by a step-parent is a sensible thing in your particular
circumstances, then the next decision is what sort of
punishment you are going to use. I can think of no
circumstances in which hitting a step-child could be
anything except extremely foolish. Physical punishment,
far from being morally reforming, is quite likely to lead to
physical injury or even death. There is no clear division
between 'legitimate' slapping and child abuse. When done
in anger, hitting a child is more likely to harm it than when
it is done in calm deliberation after the anger has subsided,
and it is hard to see how lashing out in anger at a person
who is too small to retaliate has any connection with moral
training or responsible social living. When it happens—and
it is liable to happen even in the calmest household when
frustrations build up—it is something to be regretted, not
built up into the specious legitimacy of doing a child 'good'.
Hitting a child when your anger has abated, and when you
are acting out of a thought-through sense of what a child
needs, is less likely to cause physical damage but more liable

DISCIPLINE, REWARDS AND PUNISHMENTS 111

to wreak long-term emotional damage on all concerned. The calm inflicting of physical pain is often a form of sexual perversion. It will leave long-term traces on the child who may come to associate sexual sensations with pain, and so disfigure the whole of its adult life.

There are other forms of formal punishment that serve the same ends as hitting people, in the sense that they convey disapproval, clear the air and convince adults of the soundness of their authority. I have in mind things like stopping the children going to parties (invariably leading to more grief for the adults than the children), docking pocket money (usually circumvented by a system of loans), and similar sanctions for which I should claim no high level of effectiveness. Like violence, such sanctions signify that the children are behaving in ways of which their adults are aware and of which they disapprove, but even such milder versions of punishment require the adults to be sure of the wisdom of what they are doing. It does not always follow that what the children have been doing is primarily important in terms of family relationships—the police may just have delivered a juvenile shoplifter, or the school complained about bullying—but generally, domestic sanctions relate mainly to what happens within the household, and this means that the children's behaviour needs to be considered in terms of its importance in the family's life. What has happened may mean that the co-operative life of the household has broken down, which in turn suggests that whatever system of discipline and punishment prevails is not working very well. This may be—often is—because the children are at a developmental phase that involves changing one set of ways of relating to the household and replacing it with another. This is an essential part of growing towards independent maturity, but that does not make it any easier to live with. If what is happening— which means bad behaviour—is the result of this sort of development, then punishment is obviously irrelevant.

Informal punishment is more subtle, and may in certain circumstances be more destructive. It ranges from the spontaneous losing of one's temper that results in no considered retribution except abuse, to a frosty disapproval

112 STEP-PARENTS AND THEIR CHILDREN

that hangs around for days. People who grow up in an atmosphere of disapproval directed more at their continuing weakness of character than at any specific wrong-doing, are liable to become adults with a poor sense of their own worth, troubled by a vague sense of guilt that prevents them having fun and leads to feelings of insecurity in their personal relationships. The risk is that adults who have decided that they are going to bring up their children without recourse to physical or other formal punishment are going to replace it with a system of informal sanctions that create a nasty atmosphere and will leave the child confused about what it is supposed to have done. This is hardly a sound basis for developing a sensible moral sense.

Exasperated step-parents wondering whether this book has any use except as a weapon with which to bang a few undisciplined heads may well feel that it is easy enough to talk. It is all very well for me to dismiss physical punishment as too brutal to belong in a civilised household, and to raise difficulties with alternative forms of punishment. I imagine that most people would in theory agree with what I have said, but that still leaves the question of what on earth one is to do. There are no simple rules, beyond the obvious one: that step-parents should be conspicuously light-handed in all matters of discipline and punishment, leaving them as much as possible in the domain of the biological parent until they have developed a relationship with the children that gives them the authority to discipline and perhaps punish. This authority is not the same as power, which comes from being bigger and having more money and experience, but involves the children recognising that the step-parent has a similar position to the biological parent regarding the right to decide things within the household. As in many, probably most, step-families, that state of affairs will never be reached, and any disciplinary attempts by the step-parent will be resented by the children, it follows that step-parents are in a weak position in the matter of discipline and punishment, and will have to live with this fact, and not try to get round it by wishing that they had more authority. That can be a frustrating situation to be in, and

DISCIPLINE, REWARDS AND PUNISHMENTS 113

frustration is liable to lead to impulsive and sometimes aggressive behaviour as a way out of it.

Although the idea of rewarding children for acceptable behaviour is, on the face of it, more congenial than the idea of punishment, rewarding is not without its difficulties. It is just as coercive as punishment, in that it seeks to mould children's behaviour into shapes that adults approve, and it is the means of implanting into children the values and attitudes that the parents decide. While all this is to a large extent inevitable in bringing up children, and reflects what goes on in life generally, it should not be forgotten that all this is a reflection of parental power, and controlling rewards needs to be done with extra care by a step-parent whose authority has to be earned, not taken for granted.

It also needs bearing in mind that rewards involve more than specific presents for specific actions. It may be possible to train dogs like that, but human behaviour is rather too complex to be broken down in that way. Reward, like punishment, has its formal and informal aspects. It may be appropriate to tie specific rewards to particular items of behaviour—perhaps offering a treat in return for helping with the washing up—but you cannot dismantle the whole life of the household into single pieces of behaviour. Attitudes, such as kindness and considerateness, are not always easy to pin down (though it is obvious enough when they are not there). There are other problems with relying too heavily on formal rewards. One is that they have a habit of creeping away from being special to being permanent. If you bribe a child to do something by a promise of a particular reward, you soon find yourself in a situation in which the child expects a reward every time it does that particular thing. Apart from the sheer expense of such a situation, there is a risk that children will be taught to develop an over-simple repertoire of tricks in exchange for rewards, whereas they need to develop patterns of behaviour based on self-control and self-reward, not simply on the approval of adults as symbolised in rewards.

Another problem with using formal rewards is that of using them mainly as a means of ingratiating oneself into

114 STEP-PARENTS AND THEIR CHILDREN

the step-child's favour, which involves using children as a means to something, not respecting them as human beings in their own right. It may be tempting to worm one's way into a step-child's good graces by presents that are ostensibly rewards for 'good' behaviour—albeit rather over-generous rewards—but these presents can quickly become effectively rewards for being nice, or not nasty, to the step-parent. Lavish gifts are not always the best way of gaining someone's affections, and if you start by giving presents, it is difficult to stop without the stopping being misunderstood. A step-parent who gives a generous reward to a child that helps with the washing-up, but is really trying to impress the child with the step-parent's generosity, is liable to end up with an expensive regime of bribery, involving a tariff of behaviour and prices that the step-parent may come to regret.

Informal rewards are less dramatic, but a more sensible way of moving towards domestic harmony. We are talking about achieving a domestic atmosphere that makes the household a rewarding place to be in. This is likely to come about not by seeing step-children—or indeed any children —as objects to be moulded into shape, but as individuals, with varied talents and attributes. By concentrating on the positive sides of the individual's make-up, and by admiring the individual's talents and strengths, we build up an atmosphere of approval in which the child will flourish. The child will learn, by this means, which aspects of its behaviour and character are the ones that adults like, and this will in itself be an important lesson for a child to learn, since as we saw, much 'naughtiness' is the consequence of inexperience, rather than anything more important, and selectively approving some aspects of a child's behaviour will help it grow out of this inexperience.

If a step-child lives in an atmosphere of approval, and experiences genuine admiration from its adults, it will at once learn about what behaviour is considered acceptable and be steered towards it. Discipline, in the sense of a regime of expectation and civilised behaviour, will by this means be defined and encouraged. In such an atmosphere, a child whose 'bad' behaviour belongs to the categories that

DISCIPLINE, REWARDS AND PUNISHMENTS 115

we discussed in the last section—lashing out in angry retaliation, or seeking attention from adults who seem indifferent to good behaviour, or purging some imagined guilt—will have less purpose. The causes of anger will diminish as a child's self-esteem rises, as it will do if it is held in respect; its guilt is liable to move slowly into more realistic focus, and it will be getting the attention that it needs without having to make a nuisance of itself. It would be silly to pretend that if step-parents can only generate an atmosphere of approval, then all disciplinary problems will promptly vanish. Life has a habit of turning out to be less simple then we should like, or as authors of books such as this seem to imply. It is not, for example, an easy matter to develop an admiration for a child whose behaviour is causing you trouble. It may be particularly difficult for step-parents, since the admiration that parents feel for their children is often an admiration of their own qualities that they detect in the children. We use phrases like 'a chip off the old block' in an affectionate way, and what we are really saying is that this admirable child is like me. A step-parent will not find his or her own talents and attributes embodied in a child to take pride in, nor will they have available to them the possibility of reflected glory which allows parents to take credit for a child's achievements on the somewhat vague grounds that the child must have inherited its talents from them. This may be silly vanity, but it makes it easier to admire one's own children more than those of other people, and it is not a source of admiration that is directly available to a step-parent. Step-parents have different sources of pride, and step-parents ought to be able to admire their own achievements in the children, but this is different from the proprietorial admiration that allows biological parents to approve of their children's attributes.

It is also not always easy to concentrate on approving a child's desirable qualities and ignoring its less desirable ones. Bad behaviour tends to be more obtrusive than good, and while ignoring it may in the long term cause it to fade, in the meantime there are the breakages to be paid for, the neighbours to be placated, one's own murderous temper to

116 STEP-PARENTS AND THEIR CHILDREN

be controlled, and possibly one's partner's justifications for a child's behaviour to put up with. Perhaps worst of all, there is a personal feeling of impotence to be handled, a feeling of helplessness in the face of a child's behaviour, a sense that one has no authority and that one is treated without respect. These feelings are real enough, and all that I am suggesting is that informal rewards, in the shape of an attempt to admire and approve of one's step-children, are likely to prove a more effective route to domestic harmony than becoming preoccupied with punishment. To return to a point that has constantly been made in this book, perfect families do not exist, and living with children involves putting up with a lot of behaviour that you would prefer to do without. Step-families are different only in that so many step-parents feel demoralised—and their inability to control the children contributes to this demoralisation—and because so many people expect step-family relationships to be poisonous that step-parents are often too anxious to prove everyone wrong, and go in search of the impossible.

4 The Nature of the Relationship

In Chapter 1, I suggested that step-parents should not automatically think of themselves as parents, but consider the other possible ways in which adults can live with children so as to enhance the children's growing towards maturity. We saw that there were two broadly possible roles that the step-parent might take: that of a parent, with all that the term implies, and that of a friend. These two possibilities were not mutually exclusive, but could be permutated and varied as the relationship changed with time, and as the child's needs developed. In terms of discipline, it is obviously sensible to consider one's role within the household, because one's responsibility for discipline will be determined by it. There is little sense in attempting to discipline teenage children who are close to the step-parent in age (and it is, of course, possible for a step-parent to be younger than the children). At the other end of the possible age range, an adult who acquires a step-child when it is very small will almost automatically be

DISCIPLINE, REWARDS AND PUNISHMENTS 117

cast in the role of a parent, and will adopt an appropriate stance on discipline—with maybe few difficulties specifically from being a step-parent (though plenty from being a parent).

What I have been saying about discipline may perhaps nudge some step-parents into adopting a more cautious posture on discipline, and into feeling that it might be prudent to think of oneself as a friend or brother or sister to the children, because these roles imply much less disciplinary responsibility than that of a parent. Such a decision could not be made in isolation, but it might be possible to confine oneself to a position of general support for one's partner's disciplinary stance without engendering the sort of problems that a step-parent may encounter in the matter of discipline. As I suggested in Chapter 1, the role of a friend may be more useful to a developing child or young person than a substitute or imitation parent (though these will often be useful and necessary things to try to be). If becoming heavy-handed in the matter of discipline is going to damage your chances of doing well the other tasks of step-parenting that we outlined in Chapter 2, then my feeling would be that discipline is something that is a dispensable aspect of step-parenting where there is another adult involved, whose relationship with the children is different and who can do things without causing resentment that the step-parent cannot. Children are not unruly monsters to be civilised by the coercive influence of adults—though they undoubtedly need to learn the sort of behaviour that is needed for a co-operative life. To the extent that adults have themselves learned the basis of such co-operation, then they are in a position to teach the children. Obviously, the adults in the household are fully entitled to make clear to their children what their own moral standards are, and how they think people should behave. But as children grow older, these must be presented as negotiable, something in which the parents believe, but not something to be imposed on the children at any price.

5 SOME UNPLEASANT ASPECTS OF STEP-FAMILY LIFE

Throughout this book I have tried to show that step-families both resemble biological families and are different from them. Not all the differences are in favour of biological families, since step-families have distinctive qualities that are potentially highly rewarding, but it would be foolish to argue that step-families do not also have their distinctive problems, and that they are commonly more fraught than biological families. This chapter is about some of the unpleasant aspects of domestic life that are perhaps more common, or more serious, in step-families than in biological families. Not all these unedifying matters are to be found in every step-family, and I am certainly not implying that step-families are characterised by the particular pieces of human nastiness that are discussed in this chapter. To repeat a point made in Chapter 1, the research evidence shows that step-families are on the whole successful and contented places. On the other hand, the research suggests that when step-families *do* go wrong, they are liable to be especially destructive. So although some of the issues discussed in this chapter are by no means universal, or even very common, they need to be taken seriously by conscientious step-parents and their partners who aim to be part of the contented majority rather than the destructive minority.

1 Sex
There is some evidence to suggest that girls are more at risk of being sexually abused by their step-fathers than by their biological fathers. It must be stressed that sexual abuse is by no means confined to step-families, for girls are regularly raped by their biological parents; and it must also

SOME UNPLEASANT ASPECTS OF STEP-FAMILY LIFE 119

be stressed that we are not only discussing an adult man's relationship with a teenager, for pre-adolescent girls are also at risk. The danger to step-sons is also a real one, but it is probably less serious than the risk to step-daughters, and since discussing it could distract attention from the more important danger, I shall ignore it and concentrate on how to avoid the more common risk of a step-father sexually attacking his daughter.

Any form of sexual relationship between a step-father and his daughter is almost certainly going to be extremely distressing and damaging to the girl. Even where it does not end in rape, it will involve sexual bullying. It may or may not be incest in the technical sense, but it is a disgraceful misuse of the power that parents have over their children, and may, rightly, be visited with heavy retaliation by the courts. Such moral condemnation is not especially helpful, however. Most men can presumably work out for themselves how iniquitous it would be to violate their step-daughters, yet the fact is that it happens, and the point is to prevent it. Sexual desires are not voluntary, so there is no point in getting angry about them. Repeating how deplorable one finds such behaviour is less useful than trying to work out ways of preventing the emotional and physical damage that could occur, and in practice most people manage their desires in responsible ways, and make sure that they do no harm.

It seems to me sensible for all step-fathers to anticipate that they will find a sexual component in their relationship with their step-daughters. Because the possibility of being sexually attracted to a child is so heinous, and a sexual relationship with one's wife's daughter so unthinkable, many men will fail to recognise that there is a desire building up. As a species, human beings are skilled at not seeing what they do not want to see, and a step-father may be as shocked as his victim when something that has been building up for some time, but which he has failed to recognise, suddenly spills out after a few drinks. By that time, however, the damage to the girl has been done, and no amount of remorse, nor the genuine belief that it was 'out of character' and that the man did not know how it

120 STEP-PARENTS AND THEIR CHILDREN

could have happened, will do away with the consequences, nor put right what has been done to her.

It is also prudent for mothers to keep the risk constantly in mind. Any sensible parent will realise that there are men who will find their daughters sexually interesting, and will take steps to protect them. There is now little excuse for being unaware that many men find their own children sexually attractive, and a woman with a second husband will be conscious of the risk—though she, like the man, will probably prefer to shut her eyes to the possibility and assume that it could not happen. A more sensible course is to recognise the arbitrary nature of sexual desire, to accept that it can attach itself to unlikely objects, and that the presence of young people in a household is likely to occasion sexual excitement from time to time in the older members.

There are certain indications that should alert a man that he may be putting the girl in danger. He may find himself over-ready to catch her in the bath or while dressing, when the girl is not conscious of any intrusion into her privacy, and when the presence of a man on such occasions may cause her little interest or surprise. It is the responsibility of the adult in this situation to ensure that he is aware of, and in control of, his feelings, and to monitor any growth in prurient interest in his step-daughter. At a simple level this involves respecting her privacy, and not barging in when she is in the bath, even when this has been the domestic habit. Similarly, the step-father is responsible for ensuring that any physical contact does not imperceptibly take on sexual overtones. When there is legitimate physical contact, the man may find his hand lingering, and that is the sign to take very seriously the possibility that the girl is at risk.

The first stage in dealing with this, then, is a frank acknowledgement to oneself that the unthinkable is a distinct possibility. And, to repeat, this is a possibility that every step-parent needs to consider, not dismiss out of hand as impossible. What should be done next will depend on the situation. It may be that a step-father has no option but to move out of the household, if he is unsure of his ability to control his desires. That would no doubt be a pity, but it would be preferable to the rape of a child. Usually,

SOME UNPLEASANT ASPECTS OF STEP-FAMILY LIFE 121

though, it will be possible to work out a regime that will enable the situation to be controlled. At the most obvious level, it means ensuring that 'temptation' is reduced, by limiting as far as possible the time spent alone with the girl, and when one is alone in the house with her, making sure that there is no nonsense about bottles of wine or anything else that might make the situation less easy to control.

Involving your partner in all this is likely to be a delicate matter. She is not likely to be too pleased to hear that you are harbouring sexual desires for her daughter. Even though, as I have argued, sensible mothers will be aware of the risk, for perfectly obvious reasons many women will prefer to shut out the possibility that it might happen within their own household. Faced with the recognition that the unthinkable might have happened, most women are likely to respond by becoming utterly demoralised or by incoherent anger. Your knowledge of your partner will enable you to guess at the long-term response. If the anger is capable of being turned into an energetic help with your problem, then confiding in her, however painful for you both, will have been worthwhile. If your partner's demoralisation is likely to turn into depression and despair, it may be more sensible to seek someone else's help with your situation. It is, though, a problem that involves you both and if it can be tackled jointly it becomes much easier to solve. Your partner will be able to help in ensuring that you are not left alone with the girl, to help you monitor your feelings, and generally to keep the situation under control.

Where sexual abuse does occur, the obvious explanation is that a step-father finds himself in the same household as an adolescent girl, perhaps regularly sees her partially dressed, is overcome with lust and rapes her. To the participants, however, things sometimes seem more complex. Men frequently claim that sexually-abused children have welcomed and seemed to enjoy what was happening. The possibility that a girl may actually encourage a man's sexual interest needs thinking about particularly carefully in the case of step-families. We should be clear that we are not discussing only violent physical coercion, but often a much gentler and more gradual process in which a

122   STEP-PARENTS AND THEIR CHILDREN

genuinely affectionate relationship between a step-father and a girl finds expression in physical caresses that imperceptibly become more erotic. In such a case we need to hold firmly in mind that such behaviour may be criminal, and that it will almost invariably be an act of betrayal by a step-father, whose commitment to his step-daughter's welfare involves being sufficiently responsible to control the drift from pleasing affectionateness into unacceptable sexuality. But that does not altogether dispose of the question of seductive behaviour by a step-daughter. After a specific age—sixteen in most industrial countries—it would not be criminal on the part of the step-father to respond to what he interprets as a welcome to his sexual advances, and the matter becomes one of private morality, of responsibility to the welfare of a young person. In such a case, it might help a step-father to behave more responsibly if he considered what might lie behind his step-daughter's apparent responsiveness to his sexual hints, and recognised that there could be more involved than his own sexual attractiveness.

It is by no means unknown for young women to find older men sexually attractive. Where that men is a step-father, there may be additional factors at work. Having lost one father, a girl may be very concerned to ensure that she does not lose another, and flirting with this new man may be a good way of pleasing him and ensuring that he stays around. She may be frightened of him, or be otherwise anxious to please him, and use her sexuality to make him like her. She may be angry with her mother, perhaps holding her responsible for the loss of the original household, and a good way of getting back at the mother would be to unsettle her relationship with her new man. It may sometimes happen that young women develop feelings of competitiveness towards their mothers, and set out to demonstrate their own superior sexual attractiveness by enticing their mother's lovers. Where a girl is jealous of the amount of affection being lavished by her mother on the new man, such competitiveness might perversely secure a greater share of the available affection for herself, and at the same time retaliate for the lost affection.

SOME UNPLEASANT ASPECTS OF STEP-FAMILY LIFE 123

In all these cases, any sexual attractiveness that the girl may locate in her step-father is not real, in the sense that it is more to do with her own confused feelings about her emerging sexuality and her situation than with the objective attractiveness of her step-father as a man. It is not him that she may imagine herself to find sexually attractive, in other words, but what he represents, or how she imagines him to be. This is not the basis for a real relationship, still less a justification for a step-father to yield to sexual temptation, however flattering it undoubtedly is to be the apparent object of sexual attraction of a younger person. The wise man, however, will enjoy the flattery, and perhaps be amused by it (though amused without mockery), but not take the thing seriously as having any basis in the real world.

There is another aspect of sexuality within step-households, and that is the possibility of sexual attraction between step-brothers and sisters. Where two households amalgamate, or where there is close contact between the step-children in the household and the children of the step-parent, the possibility is obvious. Many adults find something obscurely inappropriate about the possibility of such a relationship, something that they cannot quite put their fingers on but which makes them uneasy. Logically, there is no obvious objection to such relationships, which do not involve 'blood' relations, and so in theory they should be subject only to the normal caution of any teenage relationship, which involves the adults doing what little they can to make sure that hearts are not broken and that no one gets pregnant. But personal relationships are not always best thought of in logical terms, and where the idea of step-children forming adult attachments embarrasses the parents, a lot of tension could build up within the household. There is, to be sure, little to be done, beyond explaining one's misgivings to the young people as best one can—and remembering that young people need to explore the possibilities of relationships, and that they are not usually amenable to advice, or too bothered by parental objections.

124 STEP-PARENTS AND THEIR CHILDREN

2 Jealousy

Jealousy is perhaps the single most common complaint about step-families, and the thing that the members of step-families most often see as disfiguring their lives. It is not an attractive emotion, and it is usually unpleasant to experience, but it is not a straightforward feeling, and in this section it may be useful to think about jealousy in general terms, before going on to discuss its place in the lives of step-families.

The first point that has to be made is that jealousy is not confined to step-families. It is found in abundant measure in biological families as well—with the significant different that step-families expect trouble, and when they get it they put it down to jealousy, whereas biological families probably regard jealousy with more confidence, sometimes even amusement. Nor is jealousy confined to families, but occurs in most social circumstances, to the point that jealousy is as nearly a universal human attribute as we are likely to find. The widespread occurrence of jealousy may give some reassurance to people who are plagued by it in their domestic lives, and keeping it in proportion is an important element in controlling jealousy.

What is Jealousy?

Common though it is, jealousy is not a simple emotion but a bundle of feelings, and we need to dismantle this bundle in order to be clear what we are talking about. The strangled anger that has no obvious basis but causes us to lash out indiscriminately, the smouldering resentment, the irritability that makes us behave meanly, are all what we know as jealousy, but the word brings together other emotions, of which the most important are envy and possessiveness. Envy is wanting what someone else has got, possessiveness is not wanting to share what we have. Envy and possessiveness are likely to show themselves most rowdily in domestic life when they erupt in squabbles over toys, or which television programme to watch, but such squabbles are usually short-lived, and trivial enough in themselves. Their importance lies in the possibility that they symbolise a deeper resentment over the commodities

SOME UNPLEASANT ASPECTS OF STEP-FAMILY LIFE 125

(for want of a better word) that comprise the main subject-matter of domestic jealousy. These commodities are time and affection.

The image of a step-family as a place beset by angry competition over time and affection, with some people wanting more of both and others unwilling to share what they have, is not, to be sure, a very attractive one—though we began this chapter by commenting that it would be concerned with unedifying matters. Such a picture is not pretty, but it suggests a way of tackling jealousy in a moderately rational way, which is to try to devise a regime in which time and affection are shared out so as to minimise jealousy.

Time is something that few families have enough of. It is, therefore, something that has to be rationed—so much allocated for one purpose and so much for another—though the process is not usually such an orderly one in most households. Time spent taking the children out has to be scrounged from somewhere else: time spent mending one child's toy has to be found at the expense, perhaps, of helping another child with its homework. The allocation of time, consequently, comes to be seen as a means of expressing preferences—and comes to be interpreted as a parent favouring one child at the expense of another. The harassed parent, naturally, does not see it like that, and usually acts more according to the urgency of the situation than from any rational plan—which often means attending to the child who is screaming the loudest. And, inevitably, time spent mending a child's toy is time that cannot be spent kissing your adult partner, and kissing your partner may involve neglecting the broken toys.

If time is something that children want from their parents, and adults want from each other, it is obvious enough that it is going to be the subject of jealousy. People are liable to become resentful if they think someone else is getting more than their share, and they are prone to try to hog all someone's time to stop anyone else getting a turn with it. The reason why time is such an important commodity in jealousy is in large part because it stands for affection, which is the second domestic commodity that

126   STEP-PARENTS AND THEIR CHILDREN

jealousy deals in. Time is one of the most important things that a step-parent can make available to the children, because to give them time is to convey to them that you care enough to make time for them, so time and affection are not alternatives, but intimately bound together. This is why time is important in understanding and handling jealousy, because it is seen as the location of affection.

To follow my earlier breakdown of jealousy as involving possessiveness and envy, children, and adults, may envy and want the affection that they see going to the members of the family who seem to be getting too much time, and this leads to anger that another family member is getting more time and affection than oneself. On the other side, members of the family, adults and children alike, are reluctant to share the time and affection that they have secured for themselves, and become aggressive in its defence. The competition for scarce resources pulls both winners and losers into the vortex of jealousy.

It is important to recognise that jealousy, partly because it is such an unlovely emotion, is often expressed in oblique ways, and not just in direct pushing and wrangling for scarce commodities. This makes it sometimes difficult to identify. It can come out in a step-parent's irritation at some harmless behaviour on the part of a child. When pressed, the step-parent may be able to explain the irritation in perfectly rational ways, yet recognise that the irritation is disproportionate. As we saw in Chapter 4, irritation has a habit of attaching stray emotions to itself and giving them expression, and jealousy regularly finds an outlet in this way. The expression of jealousy is a highly variable matter, but it commonly needs a disguise. A small child may be sufficiently unselfconscious to push its way into time allocated to someone else, or to muscle in on overt displays of affection. When the time and attention of adults is being wasted on the meagre skills of a younger member of the household, many children will show that they can do much better what the young upstart is attempting to do, and will dance more flamboyantly, shout louder, draw more accurately and otherwise engage in what is known as showing off. This annoys adults, but it may well get their

SOME UNPLEASANT ASPECTS OF STEP-FAMILY LIFE 127

attention, if not their approval or mirth. Teenagers may engage in other forms of behaviour designed to secure attention. Adults are more likely to express their jealousy by becoming irritable or depressed. What matters is not the details, but the possibility that any particular tension or unpleasantness within the household may be the mouth-piece of jealousy.

Handling Jealousy

In dealing with jealousy, there are three things to do. The first, to pick up my last point, is to learn to recognise it, both in others and in oneself. This means acknowledging that one's life is affected by an emotion that is at once unpleasant and undignified—for it is not very 'adult' for a step-parent to experience jealousy towards a child. Learning to recognise jealousy will make sense of some of the perplexing and apparently baseless anger within one's relationships, and this in turn will go some way towards handling jealousy, for making sense of things is at least making a start towards resolving them. To acknowledge to oneself that one is resentful of the time that one's partner spends with a child may take a fair bit of doing, because one is supposed to have got over such feelings when one left childhood, but if it is there, you will only waste psychological energy trying to keep the fact from yourself. Trying to hide it from yourself means that the feeling will emerge in disguised ways—for instance, you may blame a child for resenting the time you spend with its parent, when the reality is the other way round.

The second way to handle jealousy is to recognise that it will probably never be completely eliminated. This is import-ant, because it means that you are not forever going to slip back into denying that your life is subject to a disfiguring emotion when you accept that this emotion is a part of life, and that the task is to live with it, not to hope to eliminate it and so continue to waste a lot of psychological effort in hiding from oneself that one has not succeeded.

Having acknowledged to oneself that there is jealousy present in the household, and that some of it is coming from you, and having accepted that this is a permanent

128 STEP-PARENTS AND THEIR CHILDREN

feature of your lives that is not going to be cancelled by a single effort of will, the third way of dealing with jealousy is to devise regimes that minimise the damage and corrosion that it causes. This involves attention to the two things that jealousy focuses on, time and affection. Of the two, time is obviously the more capable of rational control. You cannot easily parcel out affection, for the simple reason that most of us are fond of several people at the same time, not one after the other, and try as we might, we are not going to be uniformly fond of them all. Where, as can happen in all households, not only in step-families, it happens that someone is not especially fond of another member of the household—and this may be a permanent or only a temporary state of affairs—any damage that this is likely to do will come not from the momentary or longer-lasting lack of warmth, but in translating this lack of warmth into neglect, by not finding time for that person or by finding too much time for someone else. You cannot control the ebb and flow of your feelings, but you can control—to some extent, anyway—the allocation of time, and do a lot to make sure that your partiality is not reflected in neglect or favouritism.

One example of disposing time so as to minimise the scope for jealousy would be in the area of the children's relationship with their biological parent. The arrival of a step-parent is likely to damage the intimacy of this relationship, particularly when the adults rush too enthusiastically into creating a family; this means that the former life in which the children and the parent spent time together with no outsiders present is lost forever. It may still be possible for the biological parent and the children to preserve some of this private intimacy, but if the household tends to spend all its time together as a group, it may make sense to arrange things so that, as a matter of policy, the biological parent and the children have some time together without the step-parent. Often this will work out conveniently where the step-parent has children by a previous union and sees them away from the new home, but in other cases it may need special arrangement. Because this sort of arrangement seems to deny the unity of the new family,

SOME UNPLEASANT ASPECTS OF STEP-FAMILY LIFE 129

many adults will balk at it, feeling that it is imperative to assert the identity of the new household as a family. There are two points that need making in response to this view. The first is that the children may not be too preoccupied with interpreting their living arrangements as a family, and more concerned to secure a place where their individualities are recognised. The second is that 'family' is not an abstract idea, but a living organism, and it will develop in the manner of other living organisms, not just by an act of creation, but slowly, almost imperceptibly. The texture of feelings and loyalties that we call a family will take time to develop, and since much of this texture already existed before the step-parent arrived, it hardly makes sense to destroy it entirely in order to put together a new version.

Jealousy is something that we all have to live with. We can do this in part by recognising that it exists, and that it is a corrosive force within the home, and in part by trying to understand it so as to learn to recognise it when it behaves mysteriously. We need to retain the knowledge that it is not a rational thing, and can erupt in the most unlikely circumstances. We need to resist the idea that our lives are ever going to be completely free of it, and keep in mind that jealousy is something to be managed rather than abolished. Dealing with it on the basis that it relates mainly to time and affection, one of which is much easier to control than the other, we should be able to ensure that time with the children and with the other adult in the household is spent in ways that recognise the potential of time to generate jealous resentment, and try to minimise the occasion for this.

3 Favouritism

The ideal family contains no favourites. It travels its untroubled way with all its affections in easy balance, with abundant time and affection available for everyone, and all its relationships in effortless symmetry. In the ideal family there are no squabbles, nobody gets angry, there are no rivalries, everybody takes turns without rancour, and nobody sees anyone else's turn as longer or better than their own. It may all sound a little boring, but many adults would gladly put up with a bit of boredom as the price for

130 STEP-PARENTS AND THEIR CHILDREN

ending the interminable arguments about who is doing best in the competition for the rewards of family life. In contrast to the ideal family, real families have problems with favouritism—as often as not despite scrupulous efforts by the adults to be even-handed. Sometimes this day-to-day imbalance is trivial and soon forgotten, but there is little doubt that in many, perhaps most, families there grow up more permanent skews in the balance of loyalties and affections that exist in the household and, commonly, an adult will feel 'closer' to one child than to another. Sensible parents keep all this in control, and do not allow the skew to become too apparent, because that could involve a child feeling excluded, but sensible parents will not try to hide their preferences from themselves.

I argued in Chapter 1 that the ideal family does not exist, or if it does nobody in their right minds would want to live in it. This means that some form of favouritism is likely to be encountered in all families, yet there are important differences in step-families. One main difference is the difference in feeling that many step-parents have towards their 'own' and their step-children. This is something that many step-parents are deeply worried about, so it needs further discussion. It often comes to a head when step-parents become parents again, and find that the intensity of their feelings for the newborn child is not matched by their feelings for their step-children. This leads to guilt and self-criticism, but ignores a very important point, which is that most people feel differently about newborn children from the way they do about older ones. Ten-year-olds, for example, may be all sorts of things—interesting, creative, and so on—but they are undoubtedly not generally as 'sweet' (to use a nauseating expression) as very young children, and different feelings towards them are entirely appropriate. I am not suggesting that the difference in feeling towards one's 'own' child has no element in it of pride of ownership and all the other feelings that go with a sense of kinship, but it is clear that this difference in feeling is normal enough, and should not in itself be allowed to become the source of corroding guilt. A measure of different feeling towards children of different ages is both

SOME UNPLEASANT ASPECTS OF STEP-FAMILY LIFE 131

normal and appropriate, and is something that most children who have reached an age when they can work things out can appreciate.

In any case, difference in *feeling* is not something that there is any point in getting too bothered about, since we cannot bid our feelings behave themselves. It is when this difference in feeling is translated into difference in *treatment* that there are problems, and we can do something about this. (If you doubt that we have control of our behaviour, try to think how many times a day you talk to your children in ways that assume that *they* can control what they are doing.) You may, indeed, prefer the step-children to your 'own', or you may prefer a mixture, but you still have the capacity to treat them equitably.

It is worth observing, however, that a case can be made for deciding not to be exactly even-handed in one's treatment of the children. Throughout this book I have constantly suggested that it may be a mistake to rush too precipitously into designating your household as a family. Trying to establish an artificial family may involve losing important and valuable elements in the real situation because they have to be ignored to preserve the fiction that this is a conventional family. One such element is the important fact that it is possible to care for people without being related or pretending to be related to them. It may be that you have decided that you are going to make no pretence that this is a family in the conventional sense, but a living arrangement that has its distinctive history and identity, comprising relationships and networks of loyalties and affections that are not going to be sacrificed to make this arrangement look like a 'normal' family, but are going to be acknowledged, and cherished. It is possible to envisage a satisfactory step-household in which each parent had his or her 'own', and in which the strengths of these relationships, and the relative weakness of the step-relationship, were both acknowledged. Such an arrangement, provided it is carried out with goodwill, might well be more acceptable to all concerned than an attempt to jam everybody into parental and child roles that they do not in their heart of hearts believe in.

132   STEP-PARENTS AND THEIR CHILDREN

Where, however, the intention is that the household should function as nearly as possible as a family, resembling a family and being run by family conventions (and this will be more common than the decision to function as an 'alternative' domestic arrangement), the question of favouritism, and of the partiality that underlies it, have to be tackled. It will probably be a constant struggle to prevent the preference that you may feel from being translated into favouritism in treatment. There will be all manner of justifications available—as, for example, that the children's absent biological parent is weighing them down with goodies, so selectively providing goodies for your 'own' children is no more than restoring some sense of balance. Some of these excuses will be perfectly sound, and may be seen as such by the children, so it is important to make sure that they are not used to cheat, to enact your preferences under another guise. If the children are to be treated equally, then self-discipline and vigilance are going to be needed.

In this vigilance, the co-operation of your partner is, obviously, important, for he or she has just as much investment as you have in fairness, and will be better placed than you to monitor what is going on. Where both partners are committed to treating all the children equally, and to supporting each other in this, then it is likely to be that much easier, because it is not always easy to see your own behaviour objectively.

What equal treatment means in practice is not always obvious. It depends to a large extent on how it looks to the children. It certainly does not mean rigid uniformity. If, for example, you bring home a cuddly toy for your newborn child, it would be eccentric to bring home an identical toy for your teenage step-son. He would think, understandably, that you were making fun of him. Children of different ages *are* treated differently, and though this will often provoke cries of 'It's not fair', children usually learn to live with it. If you live in a household in which children are unduly sensitive to the possibility of favouritism and on the look-out for partiality, it suggests that they feel unsure of their place in the household, or uncertain about the

SOME UNPLEASANT ASPECTS OF STEP-FAMILY LIFE 133

nature of their relationships, especially with their step-brothers and sisters or their half-brothers and sisters. Since I have argued throughout this book that step-children have every reason to be uncertain of their position unless painstaking efforts by their adults are able to put their minds at rest, it seems likely that step-children will be especially prone to worries of this sort. To reassure them, one possibility would be to go in for some over-compensation, in the shape of doing more for step-children than for one's 'own', spending more time with them and generally taking more trouble. Realistically, though, the scope of such discrimination is likely to be strictly limited— there are only so many hours in the day, and the sort of demonstration of your lack of preference that would be likely to satisfy the suspicious mind of a step-child who is feeling pushed out would probably need to be too dramatic for it to be practical. A more promising way of dealing with the favouritism that a step-child is perceiving is to explore it in the terms that we have just been doing—that is to say, in terms of the different treatment and emotions that attach to different ages—and to use the discussion to show that you are aware of the feelings of being less-favoured; at the same time you should give the child the space to talk about its feelings. What is important is not to keep your ideas to yourself, but to explain the basis of what you are doing to the children. It is extremely unlikely that they will always share your estimate of justice, but if they know that you are trying to be fair, and that you are aware of the problems and the issues, you should at least be able to avoid an angry sense of grievance from building up. Depending on the age of the child, and upon its level of sophistication in understanding, it is often possible to help it to see that different treatment is primarily to do with age, and that it would not be appropriate to treat children of different ages identically. This can be tied to concrete experiences of the child, for example, bed-time: Children of different ages go to bed at different times, and an older child will readily see this as a point of discrimination in its favour; this will help it to grasp that fairness is not a matter of rigid codes.

134 STEP-PARENTS AND THEIR CHILDREN

4 Scapegoats

Virtually all groups have scapegoats, someone to blame for all that goes wrong. The process is a convenient one, ensuring that blame does not get shared around and that there is an explanation for the troubles that might otherwise become frightening because they are not understood. Families do this as much as other groups, and though in families it is often confined to friendly banter at the child who is *always* last, or at a parent who is *always* losing things, the process is by no means necessarily a good-humoured one, and it is possible for the life of the scapegoat to become utterly miserable. When anything, however minor, goes wrong in a household, if the immediate reaction is to ask, 'Where's Hamlet?' or to say, 'Look what Cinderella's done now,' then you are engaged in scapegoating.

In order to identify who, if anyone, is your personal scapegoat, imagine that you have just trodden on a roller-skate that someone has left at the top of the stairs. In such a circumstance, you have very little time, well under a second, before you hit the floor of the hall, but you have enough time to blame someone, and that someone is your scapegoat. Step-children are obvious candidates. They are often more difficult than other children because of what they have been through and because of the problems in their current situation, and they may bear an unwelcome physical resemblance to their absent parent, so reminding the remaining biological parent of a failed relationship (and of the less attractive features of the absent parent). To all this can be added the distance that many step-parents feel because of the absence of any genetic connection, which means that the step-parents can dismiss the childish incompetence that is causing so much trouble as having nothing to do with them, since it is not of their 'breeding'. It is easy to see why step-children get singled out for scapegoating.

If there is any substance in the tradition of the wicked step-parent, this process of scapegoating may be behind it. With a step-child as such a strong candidate for scapegoat, all the family's problems can be blamed on it, and the

SOME UNPLEASANT ASPECTS OF STEP-FAMILY LIFE   135

resultant harsh treatment be justified because the child is seen to behave in ways for which the rest of the household does not want to accept the blame. This, perhaps, was the function of Cinderella, the repository for all the family's shortcomings, blamed for the ugliness of the sisters and all the tribulations that made her stepmother so angry. There isn't enough food: blame the appetite of someone in the family—and who better than the step-child? Much better than accepting that it is to do with the incompetence of the adults. No husbands for the ugly sisters? Blame Cinderella, always flirting with the men and putting them off. And this castle would be a much happier place, Hamlet, if you weren't so blessed *moody*.

Scapegoating, then, is a common, perhaps even a universal, occurrence, and, to repeat, in most families it is harmless enough if it is confined to the level of affectionate banter rather than serious blame. Certainly in most families it is probably less destructive than it is in many workplaces, and in societies that blame minority groups like Jews and Blacks for all the problems that have been created by everyone. But in step-families, even more than other families, we should not allow ourselves to become complacent. This is partly because of the misery that can come with the position of scapegoat when it persists, but also because there is an allied tendency that is almost as universal as the tendency to find someone to blame for one's own failings, and that is the tendency for predictions about people to come true. If a child is depicted as, for example, someone who is always late, that child is highly likely to slip into the role that is described for it and to become an inveterate latecomer. We can see this tendency throughout life: girls become gentle and submissive because this is the role that they are cast into in life's drama, middle-class children do better at school than their working-class contemporaries because this is what is expected of them, and so on. If a step-child is allowed to occupy the position of scapegoat for too long, or too seriously, then that child may indeed start to behave in ways that fit the image, and that could be very unpleasant for everyone concerned.

136 STEP-PARENTS AND THEIR CHILDREN

Handling the problem of scapegoating is first a matter of recognising that it is happening, and assessing how serious it might be. Because it is something that happens more or less by chance, and since families do not, on the whole, make a decision about who is to be the scapegoat, but wait for one to emerge or to appoint himself or herself, then the scapegoating process develops imperceptibly, without people realising what is going on. Having recognised it, and having spotted the process and the victim, it is next necessary to work out why the victim is who it is, and what needs within the family are being met by the scapegoat. The victim may have been selected for reasons that we have touched on—that a step-child is a good candidate. The needs of the family are likely to be harder to recognise and acknowledge, because they will probably not be too creditable. Not to put too fine a point upon it, it is not edifying to blame a child for the problems with adult relationships that really stem from the adults' immaturity or inability to learn from past experiences, or to hold a child responsible for difficulties caused by your inability to manage money. But few people like to acknowledge to themselves that they have made a mess of things, and putting the blame on someone else is a good way of preserving one's own feathers adequately unruffled.

The very frequency of scapegoating should help us realise that it is a useful thing to do because it helps to meet the family's needs, and not some random or frivolous act of spite. In other words, it may be important for the family's well-being that it has a scapegoat, and when this is the case, as it commonly will be—then what matters is that the scapegoat shouldn't be too oppressed and demoralised by the role. Since, having recognised the scapegoating process it becomes harder to do it, then it also becomes that much harder to leave a scapegoated child unrescued; that is useful, but it does not meet the needs that the scapegoat is serving, and here there are two strategies. The first is to allow the role of black sheep to rotate within the family, almost as a game. One week, make a family decision to blame Hansel's untidiness for what goes wrong, the next week blame Gertrude's drinking, and so on. This process

SOME UNPLEASANT ASPECTS OF STEP-FAMILY LIFE 137

lightens the burden of being a scapegoat considerably, it makes it much harder to allow someone to slip into the permanent role, and it draws the attention of the household to the fact that things go wrong as a part of life, that they are not always someone's fault, and that when someone is to blame, it is usually a matter of group responsibility rather than of an individual, and certainly not of the same individual all the time. What may seem a game, in other words, has an important function as a means of education and as a reminder for people in the household.

A second way of shifting the scapegoating burden is to nominate someone outside the family. This is common. People blame the housing office for all their problems, or the boss, or the government or the neighbours. This can, of course, become counter-productive, leading to feuds that get nobody anywhere and work against the solving of problems, but it is much better for the happiness of everyone in the household to blame someone outside rather than someone inside the family for the things that you as a group cannot handle. And the scapegoat you have chosen will probably not be aware of the honour and will sleep untroubled by your problems.

There is a difficulty with this second suggestion. Many step-families nominate the absent biological parent for the post of scapegoat—or rather the adults do. Like step-children, such parents are strong candidates, because they undoubtedly have some responsibility for the family's troubles, and a shared dislike will bring the adults in the step-family closer together—since there are few things so cosy as disliking the same people. The problem is the obvious one of involving the children in blaming someone they love and admire, and creating tense and divided loyalties in the children. As in scapegoating within the household, therefore, self-discipline is needed in choosing alternative scapegoats if one kind of trouble is not to be replaced by another. Scapegoating meets complicated psychological purposes that have been only crudely touched upon in this section, and the importance of the process in domestic life should not underestimated. What is important is to ensure that step-children, or indeed any other

138 STEP-PARENTS AND THEIR CHILDREN

members of the household, are not made miserable to atone for all the family's troubles, or while the family casts around for alternative scapegoats, and the best way to protect people from this is to be aware of the issue and to bring goodwill and clear thinking to bear on it.

SECTION III

MAKING SENSE OF STEP-FAMILY LIFE

6 UNDERSTANDING STEP-CHILDREN

Step-children are children like any others, and it is only as sensible to make generalisations about them as it is about children in general. No two are alike, and no child is a static thing, but a creature that goes through massive changes between birth and the middle or late 'teens when it achieves independence. The word 'child' is also not static, for it means both a young human, and a person in a particular relationship with an adult, so that an elderly couple may refer to their 'child', when the person in question is over fifty. With such a preamble, it is obvious that this chapter cannot hope to provide a general picture of step-children, nor do anything except introduce some ideas that may help adult members of the household to make more sense of the younger members.

I discussed the importance of trying to understand what is going on in one's life, and within the people in it, in Chapter 1. Understanding does not in itself solve problems, but it helps to make them less frightening, because it is often the things that we do not understand that are the most difficult to live with. In the case of step-children, the two adults may be approaching them in ways that obscure understanding, and hence make the children's behaviour rather alarming. The step-parent may approach them with experience of his or her own children in mind, or with general ideas about children which can lead to unreal expectations about what is usual behaviour in young people. The biological parent may fail to realise how important the new domestic arrangement is in the lives of the children, and continue to try to understand them and their behaviour in terms that made sense before the step-parent's arrival, but which are now obsolete.

An important point to remember about all children, not

142 STEP-PARENTS AND THEIR CHILDREN

just step-children, is that they are not locked into simple two-way relationships with their parents, but have relationships with other adults and with other children that together may be as important as their relationship with their parents. This becomes ever more true as children get older, but even very young children of a year or so old will already have developed a repertoire of ways of dealing with the different adults in their lives. This needs stressing, for it is easy to slip into assuming that the presence of a step-parent is *the* most important fact in a child's life, when this may not be true. The step-parent may be only one of a number of more or less important adults in the child's world, and the step-child's behaviour and state of mind may be affected by factors other than the presence of a step-parent.

Step-children and the Experience of Loss
Of these other factors, an important one is the fact that all step-children are products of 'broken homes'. This expression includes children whose parent has died, as well as those whose parents chose to split up, and can be stretched to include children who have never lived in a two-parent household because their fathers were unknown, or disappeared before they were born. I am not suggesting that all children from broken homes are going to turn out to be delinquent or otherwise troublesome, nor that single parents are not fully capable of bringing up children successfully. What is important to consider, however, is whether any difficult behaviour is necessarily a response to the presence of a step-parent, or whether it might have to do with their experiences when their original home broke up. Step-children are sometimes sullen and mutinous, and they may be on average more difficult than other children, but this could be because of their experiences before the step-parent arrived—though of course the arrival of a step-parent can make things worse by introducing more conflicts and stress into an already difficult emotional world, and by causing the children to resent this intruder into their lives. Against that, though, is the crucial point about step-parenting, that the arrival of a step-parent may

UNDERSTANDING STEP-CHILDREN 143

be helpful in putting right some of the effects of the broken home, and step-parents should not feel that they are passively destined for traditionally hostile relationships with already difficult children. If they are to help the step-children overcome some of the experiences of the past, then trying to understand the step-child, the effects on the child of its experiences when its home broke up, and the possible consequences of the step-parent's arrival in the child's life, are all obviously important.

A central experience of step-children is that of loss. Most of them will have experienced loss in two stages, first the loss of a parent, not necessarily completely, but as someone who is a daily inhabitant of their domestic lives, and secondly the loss of certain aspects of their relationship with their remaining parent caused by the arrival of a step-parent. Even children whose father disappeared before they were born will share the second form of loss and will have experienced the inevitable pain of having to share their parent with a newcomer. With loss being such an inevitable component of the lives of step-children, it provides an obvious starting-point in trying to understand one's step-children and one's relationship with them.

The only safe generalisation when considering loss is never to under-estimate its importance. A child may show little grief, but that does not mean that it is indifferent; it may never refer to the missing parent, but that could be because it is too well-mannered to risk embarrassing a step-parent; all our common sense may tell us that a child cannot possibly remember a parent who disappeared when the child was a baby, but we do not know enough about the emotional development of babies to be confident. It is much safer to assume that the experience of loss has been of crucial importance in a step-child's life, and crucially significant in the development of its character and personality. This does not mean that a step-child (or any other child who has lost a parent) requires constant sympathy, nor does it mean that children can be allowed to dine out on their loss by offering it as an excuse for any bad behaviour or shortcoming. Surviving loss is a part of being human, and children as well as adults have to live with this bleak

144 STEP-PARENTS AND THEIR CHILDREN

fact and to reconstruct their lives as best they can—something that in practice most of them manage to do; but because, sooner or later, loss happens to everyone, does not justify robust indifference in those around the person coping with it, nor a callous pull-yourself-together heartiness. What is needed is an imaginative and unobtrusive awareness that is, naturally, much easier to describe than to achieve.

We are a society that discourages overt emotion; we admire stoicism in our children as much as in adults, and encourage them to mask their feelings. 'Don't make such a fuss,' we regularly say. In the case of loss, many people get very embarrassed in its proximity, and anyone who has experienced a bereavement will know how people unexpectedly avoid them, and how close friendships become stilted as the fear of raw emotion makes our friends uncomfortable. All this encourages children to keep their feelings to themselves or to express them in indirect ways that may be misunderstood, because a society that prefers not to look at grief will prefer to see behaviour as 'naughty' when it may actually be an expression of the child's confusion and anger that no one is prepared to notice what it is going through. In the case of a step-child, there may be an extension to the general prohibition on expressing feelings, because there may be little room to try to describe one's confusion and hurt to a parent who is totally goofy over his or her new lover, and takes it for granted that the child will share in his or her happiness. There may, in short, be no audience for a child to try to express what it is feeling, to try to make sense of the welter of emotions that may be clustering round its memories of its missing or displaced parent and its reaction to its new parent.

I do not mean to imply by all this that children are necessarily doomed to become impotent onlookers to the drama of their lives, with their feelings strangled and disregarded because they have no one to share them with. Many children have access to just the sort of imaginative and sensitive adults that they may need—their own parents or those of friends, teachers, clergymen or social workers, for instance—and they may have brothers or

UNDERSTANDING STEP-CHILDREN   145

sisters and friends who are fully in tune with them. Nor do
I mean to imply that it is necessary to discuss or describe
one's feelings to prevent them from somehow going
rancid. But what does seem clear is that the experience of
loss is bound to colour a child's relationship with its step-
parent, and that the child will have picked up society's
general prohibition on making a fuss about loss, as well as
the possible tactlessness of talking about it in the child's
particular domestic circumstances, and that consequently
the effect of loss on subsequent personal relationships will
be subtle and elusive. Understanding such an impact,
therefore, will be a matter of intuition and perhaps
guesswork rather than a process of interrogating the child
to get it to explain how it is feeling.

The nature and the impact of the loss will depend on how
old the child was when it occurred, the child's personality
and what sort of experiences it had in its life before the loss,
the circumstances of the loss and how it was handled by the
remaining adult. Each individual case is different, and these
factors will combine in subtle and shifting ways, so
discussing each factor in isolation is bound to be too simple,
but it may nevertheless be helpful and not misleadingly
simple to take them individually.

Coping With Loss
a   *The Circumstances*
The circumstances of the loss will range from the unex-
pected suicide of a parent, to the amicable break-up of a
marriage with one parent moving a couple of doors down
the street and remaining in daily touch with the children. It
may seem arbitrary to bracket such a range of experience
as a single event, so it will make more sense to discuss two
varieties of loss: those that are complete, with the death or
emigration of the parent, and those in which the loss
relates more to the domestic situation than to the person,
with whom some sort of contact remains possible. In
practice the two categories will shade into each other,
because many parents who are alive and well rapidly lose
touch with their children and, so far as personal relationships are concerned, might as well be dead; so the two

146   STEP-PARENTS AND THEIR CHILDREN

categories of permanent loss and partial loss are certainly too simple. There are, however, features of coping with loss that are likely to be crucial for a step-parent's relationship with a child, and these will be importantly affected by the circumstances.

The first of these is the common response to a bereavement of refusing, or being unable, to accept that it has happened. Because of this, it may, paradoxically, be easier to get over the loss caused by death than over the more protracted but never fully complete loss of an absent parent who drifts further and further out of your life. This is because the process of mourning a loss cannot properly get under way when there remains an element of hope— however unrealistic—that the loss is not permanent. People who have suffered a bereavement commonly take time to realise and believe the completeness of their loss. Often they will momentarily forget what has happened, though the forgetfulness can be more sustained, like laying a place at the table for the lost person, or a genuine belief that one has seen and talked to someone who is dead. How long this typical phase of denying reality lasts in bereavement will vary, as will the degree of conviction with which it is experienced, but normally it fades with time, generally disappearing as the initial shock of the loss sinks in, and the bereaved person is then free to reconstruct the world and to embark on the process of becoming reconciled to the loss and starting to live again without the absent person. This process of reconciliation and rebuilding can only begin when a bereaved person has recognised the loss for the total thing that it is; so for a child whose parent has never fully left, this process of rebuilding may not be able to start, and the phase of mourning in which the loss is denied may become a permanent part of life, with fragments of hope, however faint, conspiring to inject an element of unfinished business into life, and effectively to prevent the process of mourning from proceeding and being completed.

Where the parent remains in constant touch, and there is no question of ending the relationship with a child, all this talk of loss and mourning may seem rather over-dramatic, for only something much more nebulous than a person has

UNDERSTANDING STEP-CHILDREN   147

been lost—something of a domestic habit rather than an emotional linkage; in these circumstances there is no particular reason why a child should come to accept the finality of what has happened as a prelude to reconstructing a life around the gap, nor why a psychological wound should grow over when the damage has been so superficial. In such circumstances, regret rather than grief might seem the appropriate response, and the phase of denying the reality of what has happened a sensible recognition of what is the case rather than a delusion. But in all such variations on the theme of loss—whether the parent drifts imperceptibly into oblivion or removes so little that the loss is scarcely significant—the step-parent's arrival on the scene is capable of provoking a crisis akin to the unambiguousness of death. To the extent that there has been an element of denial, with its component of false hope and even traces of delusion, in the child's perfectly natural sense that any loss entailed in the parent's removal from the home is not necessarily permanent, then a step-parent's arrival is a major challenge to that view: the prospect of going back, of recovering the world that is lost, is irreparably jeopardised. The child's relationship with its absent parent may be largely unaffected, but its sense of having lost what it remembers of its family life is likely to be precipitated by the step-parent, and though such a loss hardly compares with the loss through death of a parent, it is a shadow of the more serious loss.

A second common feature of mourning that is bound to affect subsequent relationships with step-parents is the idealisation of the lost person. By this process, an average human being becomes sanctified in the memory of the survivors: shortcomings are filtered out in the recollection, talents and virtues are magnified. There seems to be more to this process than the familiar way in which memory tends to retain the good times and mislay the bad, for we are talking about the falsification of a memory by exaggeration as well as by simply selecting the convenient bits to remember. Idealisation of this sort is normally associated with the death of the person who is being idealised, and normally it fades with time, to be replaced by a more

148 STEP-PARENTS AND THEIR CHILDREN

balanced and realistic memory of the lost person that is actually more respectful of their memory because recalling them as real human beings to whom one could respond and relate, rather than as monodimensional fantasies. When the phase of idealisation is replaced by such warm and accurate memories, then the mourning person is in a position to develop new relationships to replace the lost one, but where the idealisation hangs on to become a permanent part of someone's life, then the rest of the human race is likely to suffer by comparison, and decent people come to seem shabby and unsatisfactory in the shadow of such perfection. When that happens, the bereaved person can become very lonely, cut off from normal human contact by the psychological barrier of unrealistic expectations, as well as by the formidable enough difficulties of making new friends and building a new life after a bereavement.

It is, of course, very much harder to idealise someone who is temporarily or fitfully absent rather than dead, because his or her inglorious reality serves as a constant check on any unrealistic tendencies towards sanctification. It is by no means impossible, though, particularly in children who have—at certain periods in their lives—a tendency to hero-worship and otherwise excessively admire a parent. Such hero-worship is naturally highly gratifying to the parent (who will do well to make the most of it, for it does not last long), but it can get entangled in the parents' troubles with their own relationship, and then it can leave the child with a horrible choice—either to accept that the greatly admired parent is all too human, or to cling, however unrealistically, to the hero-worship. Most people are capable of hanging onto ideas no matter how strong the evidence to the contrary may be, and so with children it may be necessary to cling to an idealised view of a missing parent because the alternative of recognising the parent's fallibility and shortcomings may be unbearably confusing and painful. When this happens, a parent who is merely absent can become canonised in much the way that dead people are.

In either event, such an idealised person is a difficult act

UNDERSTANDING STEP-CHILDREN 149

to follow, and a step-parent moving into a family where such idealisation exists is going to have to be patient, and in particular to control a natural exasperation that the child cannot perceive how much more desirable this new parent is than the one who is being idealised. It would be extremely foolish to attempt to argue a child out of its idealised picture of a missing parent—foolish because it is not a rational process that can be dispersed by reason, and because it is likely to lead to resentment and to attitudes becoming ever more entrenched. For a step-parent to attempt such arguing could be disastrous, for although children are not particularly likely to spell it out, this interloper is suffering very badly by comparison with the idealised parent, and if the new parent gets involved in behaviour that is genuinely rude and tactless, such as criticising a parent, then the unfavourable comparison is likely to become firmly fixed. You cannot expect a child to give up its memory or perception of a cherished parent because you do not share them, and all that an incoming step-parent can do is to allow time to do its work, for the idealised picture to fade into something nearer reality, and for a relationship with the children to unfold as the children perceive the new parent's real qualities, unencumbered by false comparisons.

It seems, then, that a complete loss, such as through bereavement, may cause less damage to a child's subsequent relationship with a step-parent than a partial loss of a parent through separation or divorce, because such a permanent loss allows the process of mourning to run its course and for time to do its healing work. Where the loss has never had to be acknowledged, there is every chance that it will be entangled in the process of forming a relationship with a step-parent. In this view, I should make it clear, I disagree with a number of other writers on the theme, and perhaps with common sense, and I should not wish to be misunderstood as implying that a child whose parent has died is in some ways more enviable than one whose parent has left, because obviously that cannot be the case. But though the permanent loss of a person is of a different order from the loss of a domestic usage, in terms

150 STEP-PARENTS AND THEIR CHILDREN

of a step-parent arriving on the scene, it may be simpler to be succeeding a dead parent than one who is living round the corner and whose place in the children's emotional life is more ambiguous.

b *The Child's Age*

A child's age at the time of a loss or bereavement is obviously an important element in how it is affected. In practical terms, older children have a greater ability to influence events than younger ones and will, for example, be in a position to keep alive a relationship with a parent who has left home, while younger children may be largely or wholly dependent on adults to make such arrangements. Similarly, the older a child, the more likely is it to be able to make sense of what has happened. This cuts both ways, for a very young child is likely to be bewildered and frightened by something that it cannot explain, and as a result may be more distressed than an older child who understands better; but the same small child may be sheltered from the full impact because it has no clear sense of the future and hence little grasp of the finality of death or the impending changes in its life, though these may be all too poignantly apparent to an older child. So rather than say that it is easier to cope with loss at one age than another, it is more sensible to recognise that the loss of a parent will have a different quality according to age, and that it should always be regarded as a serious matter.

One thing that teenagers will not usually meet is the assumption that they are too young to understand or to know—rather the opposite, in fact, for teenagers are commonly invited to take sides in their parents' matrimonial difficulties, which suggests that teenagers are often assumed to understand much more than they actually do, and that they are more sophisticated than their bewilderment at what is happening in their lives might suggest. But it is often assumed about small children that they cannot be expected to understand and as a result not enough notice will be taken of the incomprehensible experiences that they are undergoing, nor of the devastating impact on the limited repertoire of their daily experiences that losing a

UNDERSTANDING STEP-CHILDREN 151

parent is going to have. There may be little sign of inconsolable grief—small children are, after all, used to people coming and going in their daily experience, and used to being distracted when they appear distressed; but they can distinguish individuals from a very early age, and surprisingly quickly develop a strong enough sense of time and place to know that this is the time of day that something usually happens and to get worried if it does not. They may not be able to describe their feelings, but that is a very different thing from not knowing that there is something going on, and anyone who has lived with pre-school children will know how foolish it is to underestimate what they know and the extent of their understanding. The fact that they cannot express their feelings in words is more to do with the inadequacy of their vocabulary than with the range or the importance of their experience, so inheriting a step-child that lost its natural parent when it was very small does not mean that it was unaffected by the loss. Even when a child is too young to have any direct memories of its parent, or to have identified the gap in its life left by the parent's departure, it will almost certainly have been aware of—and affected by—the distress that its parent or parents were feeling, and in its turn experienced distress because of this contagion. Moreover, no matter how well organised and conscientious the parents are, the departure of one of them will be bound to upset the domestic regime, and many children are particularly involved in their routine and liable to be very bothered by its disruption. This has to be stressed, because parents who have split up have a vested interest in minimising the importance of any damage they might be doing to the children.

A fragment of observation is worth offering. It is incapable of being scientifically tested, but it may help some parents understand an otherwise puzzling moodiness in their children. It is noticeable how important annual anniversaries are to some people. Anniversaries do not only include identifiable dates to celebrate, like birthdays, but more nebulous associations with particular times of years. Our moods can be affected by the half-remembered experiences of the same time of year in the past, because

152 STEP-PARENTS AND THEIR CHILDREN

the passage of the seasons is marked fairly precisely by innumerable natural and artificial signs—the blooming of daffodils or the appearance of the municipal Christmas tree, for example. The distinctive signs and smells, together with the length of the day and the temperature, bring to mind days from the same time of the year in the past, though one may not have noticed them in the calendar. For years after leaving school, many people are anxious when certain summer days remind them of exams, though they may not consciously make the connection, and be aware only of a vague unease left behind from school days. Other people may experience the same vague nervousness that they felt at the beginning of each new academic year when early autumn reminds them of it, though without necessarily bringing it consciously to mind. Such anniversaries may be particularly significant in the lives of people who have had an experience of major importance in their lives before they had developed the intellectual equipment to explain it. They will sometimes become unaccountably distressed as the time of year reminds them of what it was like to live with a distressed parent whose own pain and grief were unequivocally communicated to the child. With children, such anniversaries may go some way to explaining why a child suddenly starts behaving in ways that are not obviously triggered off by events in its immediate life. I make no strong claim for this insight about anniversaries, and it is obvious enough that if you start looking for odd moods in a child at a time of year that you would expect it to have unhappy memories, then you will almost certainly find them; but for children who had a devastating experience before they were in a position to explain it, such anniversaries may provide a clue to untypical behaviour when they are older, and make it a little easier to live with the child—particularly if there is a reasonable chance that the mood will fade as the anniversary does.

An important variation in a child's response to loss is how responsible it feels for what has happened, and this is closely related to age. Generally, the younger a child is, the more it is liable to think that what has happened is its own fault, and consequently the greater its sense of guilt. Some

UNDERSTANDING STEP-CHILDREN 153

small children are burdened with a major sense of their own responsibility for events in their world. This so-called 'magical thinking' gradually fades as children learn a more sophisticated sense of cause and effect and come to realise that most of the things that happen in the world are unaffected by them, but younger children may genuinely believe that their naughtiness has caused a catastrophe: the panic reaction that 'I've done it now' is common when some disaster coincides with an actually unrelated episode of persistent bad behaviour. In part, of course, parents often induce this disproportionate sense of responsibility by threatening not to love a naughty child or blaming it for all sorts of things in an exasperated attempt to make it see that one is serious in wanting it to stop doing something and behave sensibly. Even in more rational households, where such hysterical behaviour is unusual, children may still hold themselves responsible and believe that Mummy or Daddy has gone away because they were naughty.

Such thinking is to a large extent inevitable when a child's developing moral sense has no other theatre than the narrow world of its immediate family, but for many people, this way of thinking never wholly disappears, and they will regularly feel some personal responsibility for causing events that were really nothing to do with them. This is common in bereaved people, who often feel that someone's death is in part their fault: 'If only I hadn't talked so much she wouldn't have had to hurry and been involved in an accident', or 'I should never have let him go'. Such exaggeration of the importance of minor events is a common feature in the shock of loss. With older people there is usually enough experience of life, and enough understanding of how things work, for that sort of guilt to gain a sense of perspective as the shock fades with time, but for younger people there is a danger of a persisting sense of guilt which will not readily disappear. It is important to remember this when trying to understand how some particularly sensitive child has responded to the disappearance of a parent, because it is too easy to assume that children have the same capacity to get things into perspective as adults, and to forget that they lack both the

154 STEP-PARENTS AND THEIR CHILDREN

experience and the knowledge to deal with their exaggerated sense of responsibility.

c *How Adults Handled Things*

The surviving adult's response to the child at the time of loss will obviously have been important in how the loss affected a child. Even more important, though, will have been the longer-term attitude of the surviving parent, because irreparable psychological damage is seldom done by a single conversation, though it can be caused by sustained mishandling. The ideal is to talk carefully and sensitively about the loss, allowing the children's understanding to develop at each one's own pace, so that each is clear about what has happened, secure in its relationship with both parents, whatever the state of *their* relationship, and confident that its feelings are understood and esteemed. It is, alas, seldom like that outside text books and agony columns, and the reality is more often a catalogue of evasions, white lies, jealousy and the neglect of legitimate feeling. It is an aspect of our lives in which many of us may have much cause to reproach ourselves.

A step-parent is usually dependent on information from the natural parent in trying to understand how a step-child's experience of loss may have affected it, and this requires a painful exercise in honesty on the part of the natural parent in describing and evaluating how he or she helped the children cope with the loss. If the natural parent feels safe and confident enough with the step-parent, it may be possible to discuss the child's loss, and the surviving parent's handling of it, so as to give both adults a clearer grasp of how it all might have felt for the child and how the child's subsequent emotional development and personal relationships might have been affected—and how they might be improved. Such clear-sighted honesty is beyond most of us, even to ourselves, let alone in what amounts to a confession to someone whose good opinion is vitally important, particularly if a natural parent has been left less confident in personal relationships by the loss of a previous partner. We are all understandably anxious to minimise the importance of our own behaviour when something has

UNDERSTANDING STEP-CHILDREN 155

gone wrong, and as often as not prone to forget the details of a painful experience. Even when the loss of the other parent was the result of death, rather than of an angry collapse of a relationship, a parent may have been too engrossed in grief to give much attention to the needs of the children, and may subsequently feel too embarrassed at such a failure to be able freely to describe all this to a new partner. So the step-parent will need imagination in fumbling towards some understanding of how step-children's experience of the loss of their natural parent may have affected later relationships—an understanding that it is essential to attempt, no matter how tentative and incomplete it may be.

While on the subject of the sort of honesty that is easier to admire than to achieve, it is perhaps the place to mention an understandable but not very helpful tendency, the reluctance to accord to his or her predecessor a realistic and fair degree of importance. A natural sense of rivalry towards the biological parent as one attempts to forge a relationship with one's step-children can lead to a wish to deny his or her significance in the lives of the children. This is especially important when the natural parent is alive and visible, perhaps seeing the children regularly and well known to the step-parent; the natural reaction to deny that such an emotionally impoverished and generally unsatisfactory person could have any real importance in the children's lives is hard to resist, because the threat to the development of one's own relationship is cogent and obvious, and the rivalry clear. But the fact that a step-parent may have a vested interest in minimising the importance and achievements of a predecessor does not mean that the loss was any less painful to a child; it may be building up a store of trouble if one fails to try to see the missing parent through the child's eyes, and to understand what his or her absence means to the child, assuming instead that the child shares one's own understandable, and possibly correct, summing up that it is better off without the missing parent. The responsibility for how a child was helped to cope with its loss is not solely confined to the natural parent, then, but is affected by such attitudes

156 STEP-PARENTS AND THEIR CHILDREN

in the step-parent; so it is not just natural parents that need to attempt the difficult honesty of estimating how helpful or unhelpful they have been to the child in its loss, but the step-parent as well.

A step-parent's understanding and appreciation of the child's loss will, then, be at best imperfect, and the light that the understanding sheds on the relationship between them will be similarly partial, but it is possible to select a few aspects of the handling of events that might have affected a child's response to the loss—and where the departing parent was in a position to talk about the situation with the children, such conversations will also have been important. The first likely event is that the parent or parents were so preoccupied with their own loss that there were not enough emotional reserves left for the children, whose feelings were as a result disregarded. It would, I imagine, be unusual for parents to be so engrossed in recrimination or grief that there was no comfort or attention available to the children, but it is the quality of this attention that is likely to have been affected—most likely by a too easy optimism that 'she's taking it better than I thought', or 'he's too young to understand'. It is in such a climate that a child might develop the fantasy of being responsible for what has happened, because it finds itself in an unfamiliar emotional world with nobody taking much real notice of it, and left to make what sense of things that it can: in such a case, a child may have to fall back on such concepts as it happens to possess in order to understand what is going on, and the notions of naughtiness and punishment may suggest themselves. A parent who is fully engaged in the business of being a parent would probably be able to spot such an absurd set of ideas developing in a child's head and deal with them by gentle reasoning and reassurance, but a parent immersed in private grief is often not fully engaged, and consequently less sensitive to a child's getting hold of the wrong end of the stick and slipping into self-recrimination and misunderstanding. Similarly, painstaking explanation, done over a longish period to allow the children to grasp difficult and painful ideas at a speed that allows them to be assimilated

UNDERSTANDING STEP-CHILDREN 157

gradually, is liable to be crowded out by the parents' self-absorption, or to be replaced by a single session of curt explanation that can leave the children with innumerable questions that have had no time to be properly formed, let alone answered, and can add up to a legacy of uncomprehending pain in which fear and bewilderment consort. The problems here may be made worse by a child's diffidence and good manners, for it may perceive the preoccupation and distress of its parents and be reluctant to intrude out of a wish not to make the suffering worse, or a fear at the possible reaction; such hanging back may go unnoticed by the parents who are wrapped up in their own problems. (The long-term legacy of this sort of diffidence can become an unproductive secrecy in which parents and children collude to avoid raising painful matters, so that children never really know what is going on in the family and end up living in nervous fear.)

A child's feelings may have got lost at the time of a bereavement, therefore, and the child may move onward through life with a freight of misunderstanding and a welter of incomprehensible distress. When this has happened, the signs of it may subsequently surface in attitudes to parent or step-parent that may make little sense until it is realised that the child may have opinions about adults—and in particular parents—that are the result of the confusion left by the loss of the original natural parent. To take again the example of a child who blames itself for what has happened, it could be that adults come to seem cruel and unforgiving if they are capable of such savage revenge, and subsequent relationships may slip into patterns caused by such a belief, so that a step-parent could find himself or herself viewed with fear or an inappropriate wish to please because such was the way that the child had much earlier worked out to avoid retaliation. Such a response to a step-parent is not based on a real apprehension of the individual person involved, and may become increasingly bizarre if that person is in practice good humoured and tolerant and too mild-tempered to get cross with a dog, let alone inflict pain on a child, but who nevertheless gets cast by a child into the role of a vindictive deity to be lied to and placated;

158 STEP-PARENTS AND THEIR CHILDREN

in such circumstances, the key to the bizarre response of the child could well lie in the sort of experience at the time of the loss of the natural parent that we have been discussing.

Occasionally there may, sadly, be some substance in a child's fantasy about causing the loss: not, except very rarely, because a parent has left as a result of the child's behaviour, but because the remaining parent may actually hold the children responsible. It would be rare for a rational adult to blame a child for the death or the departure of a partner, but it is far from rare for families to engage in elaborate rituals of scapegoating a member of the family, and holding him or her responsible for all that goes wrong; a fuller discussion of this process of scapegoating has been given in Chapter 5; here it is mainly important to recognise that a child who is accustomed to be blamed for everything is likely to take some of the blame seriously, and not to realise how arbitrary the process of becoming a scapegoat is, nor how primitive is this way of explaining a family's troubles, by putting the blame for complex mismanagements and misunderstandings in family relationship at the feet of a single participant. Yet if a family is engaged in such scapegoating—and most families do at some stage—then it follows that a child who holds itself responsible for the loss of a parent is not totally misjudging the situation.

A further problem in handling a child's experience of loss is that there may have been around at the time that it happened a lot of anger and recrimination, with associated vilification of the departed parent to the captive audience of children remaining. There are, almost invariably, faults on both sides when a relationship comes to an end—or indeed, no faults at all in a relationship that has simply worn out—and sensible people aspire to an amicable break, free of recrimination and based on an adult recognition of mutual incompatibility, good wishes and no hard feelings towards each other and a frank and open explanation of what has happened to the children, couched in terms of affectionate regret and self-deprecation. Such a highly civilised state of affairs is usually so short-lived that its only importance is as a stick with which the warring parties

UNDERSTANDING STEP-CHILDREN 159

can beat each other as alleged breaches in the cordial truce take their places alongside the catalogue of shortcomings and unpleasantnesses of one's erstwhile partner. In the less heroic world that most of us inhabit, it is highly likely that the children will be invited, however subtly, to take sides in the disputes of their parents, with a twofold consequence: the first is the sort of neglect of the children's feelings that I have already described—the crowding out of what they are experiencing because of the urgency of their parents' mutual dislike.

The second is more complex, and relates to the process of idealising the lost person that was discussed earlier. In this process, very ordinary people become saints, their short-comings forgotten, their merits exaggerated as the bereaved person venerates their memory with only a slim grasp on reality. Normally this fades with time, and I argued earlier that it was something that was likely to have a different quality, and to pose different problems, depending on whether the loss was the result of death or of separation, for it is likely to occur in a much less rampant form when there is a powerful limitation to the process of idealisation —such as when the lost person is to be seen every evening wending his drunken way to his new home. But though it occurs only in a shadowy form when a home has been broken up, such a form is common, and almost certainly will have been missed by the remaining parent who would probably be hard put to identify a single merit in his or her former partner, let alone make much sense of the idealised view that the children may be beginning to harbour. If, as is common, the children are being invited to share the unflattering view of the other parent, they are liable to be terribly muddled by the two competing tendencies— towards idealisation and towards accepting the opinion of the person who is caring for them. This muddle is likely to be made even more confusing if the idealised parent is also engaged in vilifying the partner who is now caring single-handedly for the children. To call this mishandling by the parents is to attach blame when it is hardly useful, and in terms of an incoming step-parent what matters is less that mishandling may have occurred, because that is the

160 STEP-PARENTS AND THEIR CHILDREN

business of the natural parents, but the legacy of confusion about adult relationships that the step-children may retain.

When discussing how a step-parent might handle this idealisation, I suggested that there was little to be done except to be patient and to try not to make things worse, which will be likely to happen if a step-parent makes any of four possible mistakes in dealing with a child's idealisation. First, a step-parent might fail to respect the children's view of their own parents (and I take the view that children's opinion of their natural parents is their business and not that of the step-parent). Second, an adult might not realise that these forces are at work in the new relationship, and in particular how the children's perception of their new step-parent may be distorted by comparison with the natural parent. Third, by ignoring the inevitability with which distance lends enchantment to a view, step-parents can allow themselves to become irritated or disappointed at not being welcomed more wholeheartedly. Finally, it is all too easy to get sucked into disparaging the absent parent in an exasperated attempt to inject a little reality into the situation. This whole area is a good example of how some measure of understanding of what is going on can make it, not easy, but easier, to avoid the sort of mishandling that could have serious consequences by trampling flat-footedly over your step-children's sensibilities, when thought and understanding might help you to generate the patience that is the only real solution to the sort of human dilemmas we are talking about.

d *Other Factors Affecting the Impact of Loss*

The most important factors affecting the impact on the child of losing a parent are those we have already discussed—the circumstances of the loss, how it was handled by the adult participants and the child's age. The exact ways in which these combine together will depend on the child's personality, and on the nature of the family life before the break—its cohesiveness, security, contentment and openness, the measure of support available from brothers and sisters. It may be, for example, that the family was a place of strife that greatly improved when the

UNDERSTANDING STEP-CHILDREN 161

natural parent left the scene—and it is a reasonable bet that the surviving parent will either take such an optimistic view, or the exact opposite and look back with unrealistic nostalgia to the golden age of family life with the absent partner—and also a reasonable bet that both accounts of the past are exaggerated. It may be that one child was so sensitive that it will have been devastated, while its more equable brother or sister was largely unaffected by what happened. It could sometimes be that a highly emotional child who evinced noisy grief at the loss is in fact someone of relatively shallow feelings who will quickly get over it, while its more phlegmatic brother or sister apparently accepted things with glum stoicism that turned out to mask a deep and enduring anguish. The approximate way in which personality and circumstances interacted, at the time of the loss and later, will only become understood by a step-parent after careful and courteous attention to the children has begun to yield glimpses into their personalities. It is not something that can be hurried, for all that such an understanding is critical in getting some grasp of what is going on in the unfolding relationship with the step-parent, and for all that the process of understanding will be masked by, and itself mask, the developing relationship. We are required as a part of being human to ponder the imponderable, and you will find no more puzzling and peremptory task than this in the whole field of personal relationships.

Another factor influencing the effect of loss is what happens in the world outside the family. In social terms the most common consequence of a family breakdown is not a rash of juvenile delinquency or psychiatric problems but poverty: a decline in living standards that may not be dramatic—though often it is—but in the medium and long term can be severe. There is almost bound to be some drop in living standards in cases of break-up (though there is sometimes a spectacular improvement when a well-insured partner dies) because the cost of maintaining the departed parent's new home will probably have to be found from the same-sized budget as before. For some children there is a humiliation in such a drop in living standard,

162   STEP-PARENTS AND THEIR CHILDREN

though it is just as likely that the children will be affected by the mood of the surviving parent who is worried sick about money as he or she looks at the budgeting for the new status of a lone parent.

And how does one tell one's friends that one's parent has left? It is now a common enough occurrence, of course, but for all that not an easy thing to announce in the playground, where there may be more jibes than sympathy to be had. Teachers are notoriously interested in such matters and will be eagle-eyed in their watch for slipping attendance or deteriorating work in a child that they have probably hardly noticed before; so a child may feel uncomfortably under surveillance at a time when it would rather have a period of anonymity than intrusive concern. Children whose parent has died can expect an element of embarrassment in the concern of their teachers, and in all probability will be avoided by their contemporaries who are afflicted by the common human fear of pain and mutilation. Older children may have more structures in their lives that will enable them to maintain a routine that minimises the problem, younger children may be less put out by the public announcement of the change in their status; nevertheless it is not an easy time, and the increased truancy rate among children following the break-up of their parents' marriage should alert us to the problems of the social consequences of loss.

There are usually other family relationships that will be affected by the loss of a parent and will themselves affect its impact. Chief among these will be relationships with brothers and sisters, and relationships with grandparents, aunts and uncles. In the case of brothers and sisters, the loss may involve factors that pull in opposite directions: there may, for example, be a tendency for brothers and sisters to become closer as they share the experience of grief when normally they have little in common, but at the same time they may find themselves in competition for the limited amount of emotional support and consolation available from their parents who are locked in their own troubles. The consequence can be a sharpening of the rivalries and jealousies that are common enough in

UNDERSTANDING STEP-CHILDREN 163

families. The disappearance of one member of a household cannot but force a remaking of what goes on in the family, of the power structure, the alliances and rivalries and the pecking order that family interactions throw up. The arrival of a step-parent throws a further spanner in the works and forces a further remaking of the family structure, and is liable to set off again the turmoil in relationships among brothers and sisters—though whether these are improved or damaged by the new arrival will depend on the step-parent's personality and approach as well as on what has gone before.

From grandparents there will, if they are wise, be a source of support that will have a particular importance from the special nature of the relationship with a grand-parent that often develops—an intimacy and a tolerance that comes from long acquaintance with an adult who feels closely associated with a child but does not have the unpleasant responsibilities of its upbringing. Grandparents are imperfect people, however, and are likely to be sucked into the tribulations of the son or daughter's marriage, and to take sides in a dispute that is almost certainly none of their business. This in its turn will get tangled up in their relationship with their grandchildren. The whole issue of grandparents and step-children was explored in Chapter 3, and what matters here is the influence that grandparents may have on a child's experience of loss. If a child is lucky, its relationship with its grandparents can be the most stable area in a world of shifting emotions and experiences, a major mitigation in an unpleasant business; if it is unlucky, it may have lost something or all of its relationship with a grandparent, and the loss of the parent will be compounded. Many children face a determined silence at the time of loss, a marked unwillingness on the part of many adults in their lives to offer the support and encouragement that they need. There is a contrast here between losing a parent through death, when adults will on the whole behave sympathetically and helpfully, and losing a parent through separation, when many adults will behave as if nothing has happened, because they are too embarrassed to talk about it.

164 STEP-PARENTS AND THEIR CHILDREN

With the loss of a parent, some children will lose the home. I have been taking it for granted that the domestic environment has not been affected in the physical sense by the loss of a parent, but this may not, of course, have been the case, and the loss or impairment of a relationship with a parent may be made worse by the loss, partial or complete, of one's home. It may, for example, be impossible for a widowed parent to keep on the family house, perhaps because it is too big, or expensive, or has too many memories. It may have been to escape a violent man that a woman has had to take herself and her children to a refuge and sacrifice the home as the price of safety. Less drastically, a departing parent may insist on taking some of the furniture and, perhaps worse, taking the family cat or dog, and though the bricks and mortar of the home may be unaffected, the child's sense of loss could be greatly increased. When trying to understand what happened to a child at the point when it lost its natural parent, and how these experiences have affected its subsequent life—particularly as it impinges on a step-parent—it pays not to underestimate the importance of such losses to a child. To a woman who is escaping a violent man, abandoning a few sticks of furniture and a mortgaged house may be a modest price, and although obviously inconvenient, replacing a home may seem the least of her problems; but many children are much more committed to objects and places than their parents, gaining some of their security from rituals and possessions. This is why small children like to take a part of their home with them wherever they go, usually in the form of a toy or blanket, and why they get unaccountably 'homesick' when away. Even in the case of a dramatic flight from a violent parent, children will almost invariably have been able to rescue something of the home, but they may be sacrificing a lot that has a significance for them that goes well beyond strictly utilitarian reasons, and makes the loss all the more brutal.

Finally there is the delicate matter of the step-parent's involvement in the loss of the natural parent. As often as not, of course, he or she will be completely uninvolved, knowing none of the parties at the time of the loss, but

UNDERSTANDING STEP-CHILDREN 165

there will be times when he or she will know the people involved, and be directly involved as a member of the eternal triangle or quadrangle that was involved in the break-up of a relationship. Even in cases where there was no involvement, it is unwise to assume that the children either know this or believe it, for children, like the rest of us, are on the look-out for explanations of puzzling questions, and are liable to jump to the conclusion that the break-up of their parents' marriage is the fault of the step-parent. Such a belief is bound to affect relationships, presumably for the worse, and where there *was* an involvement that the children, knowing nothing of the delicate passions of their elders, might see as culpable or sordid instead of tragic or noble, then step-parents will do well to tread very cautiously. To put it bluntly, if you have run off with someone else's partner, then you have some explaining to do to the children whose home and life have been disturbed, and they are not very likely to see the thing in the same way as you do. No doubt you think they are much better off with the step-parent than with the parent that he or she usurped, but small children do not like people who make their parents cry, and older children do not like people who might seem to be making them ridiculous among their friends. It pays, therefore, to be tentative in your estimate of how enviable their present lot has become, of how unsatisfactory their previous parent was, and how misunderstood one is in the role of a homewrecker.

Children and Innocence

There is a final version of loss that relates not to a person nor to a situation, but to something much less tangible though nevertheless important. Many step-children will have lost their sense of how the world is. They may have been forced to relinquish a sense of security when the wall of affection and care was suddenly breached by the death or disappearance of a parent, and once breached there can be no recovering the total protection of that wall. When the home was disbanded with acrimony, they may have been forced to abandon their assumptions about how adults, and particularly their parents, behave. But whatever the

166 STEP-PARENTS AND THEIR CHILDREN

details, children who have lost a parent will almost certainly have lost in the process some of their understanding of how things are. To the extent that we are talking about childhood innocence, then obviously most people must lose it sooner or later and come to realise that life itself is impermanent, and that within life personal relationships are fragile and human behaviour is regularly unattractive; for myself, I take no pleasure in such realisations, so it seems to me better that children should be protected for as long as is responsibly possible from such sombre recognitions, and wrong to take lightly their premature exposure to the facts of adult existence. We are, let us be clear, talking about something much more serious than the existence of Father Christmas when considering what illusions the loss of a parent may force a child into giving up, and some sensitive and thoughtful children will mourn the loss of a belief (even a misguided one) almost as keenly as they will mourn the loss of something tangible, and be just as sad and angry. There is a view of childhood that sees it as a steady aggregation of such losses, and explains adult behaviour as the expression of the pain and rage at the process of loss: that may seem an unduly sentimental account of the matter, but to the extent that it highlights the importance of defending childhood innocence, it deserves to be taken seriously.

Children who have experienced such a sense of loss, and been unusually taken aback by it, may become subdued, even depressed, which brings with it a liability to daydreaming as a way of avoiding the present reality. This carries a consequent risk of impaired school performance, or anger at adults who have shattered the image they once held, which may in turn show itself as 'bad' behaviour that makes sense only in terms of lashing out indiscriminately as a means of venting an intangible but unmistakable sense of grievance, brought on by lost illusions. Adults who have got used to living in the 'real' world may find such a serious view of childhood's shattered illusions a little fanciful: but confronted with otherwise inexplicably disruptive behaviour, such a view may become more convincing.

7 UNDERSTANDING THE ADULTS IN STEP-FAMILIES

In the last chapter we looked at some of the factors that might be useful in trying to understand step-children. This chapter is concerned with the adult members of the household, and with exploring aspects of their situation so as to highlight some of the particular problems and strains that go with being an adult in a step-family. By thinking about their situation, and that of their partners, adults can perhaps start to put together a picture of how difficult this situation is, to begin to work out some of the dynamics of their own unique circumstances so as to see whether they need changing or adapting, and make a realistic assessment of how 'well' they are doing as adults in a step-family.

Hopes, Expectations, Misgivings and Fears

Before considering the individual circumstances of the step-parent and the biological parent in a household, it is worth thinking a little more about what we might call the nature of second marriages of people with children. In the Introduction to this book, I suggested that the research evidence did not bear out the general pessimism that exists about step-families, and indicated that they are capable of being just as satisfactory places in which to bring up children as biological families. It remains true, nevertheless, that step-families have a bad image, and it is also true that most adults set up step-families with hopes and expectations that are rather different from those of couples contracting a first marriage (or a marriage without existing children).

People get together on a permanent basis for all sorts of reasons, but it is unusual for children to be a positive asset in a potential partner. It is certainly not unknown for someone to be looking for a person with children, as the lonely-hearts advertisements in the press show, and it is

168 STEP-PARENTS AND THEIR CHILDREN

likely that someone's treatment of his or her children will
often attract a possible partner who sees it, but normally
the children will be, at best a more or less acceptable
inconvenience, at worst a major drawback. There is often a
lot of jokey consolation to be found in having a 'ready-made
family', but the fact is that becoming a step-parent
represents a variation on what most people regard as the
normal way to do things. The normal way is supposed to be
that boy meets girl, they fall in love and live happily ever
after. It hardly ever happens like that, but the dominant
ideal in western countries is for two single people to choose
each other. When one or both partners have children from
previous relationships, there is clearly a major departure
from the conventional arrangement—and it is worth
stressing that though there are now plenty of step-families
about, they are still a small minority of families. The
practical consequences of an arrangement being unusual
may not turn out to be important, but it can also give to a
relationship an unpleasant 'taste' that is not easy to
dismiss, and which may affect morale and the family
atmosphere in general.

For potential step-parents there is first the social
embarrassment of explaining to friends and parents what
is happening. This is likely to be easier if you have children
yourself, but it may not be by any means easy if you have
not. Many parents, in particular, brought up in an age
when marriages were less easy to dissolve, may find the
existence of the potential in-law's children slightly embarrassing, or even feel that it spoils the whole thing. If you
have been saving up all your life to give your daughter a
white wedding, you hardly had in mind her fiancé's
children among the bridesmaids, and if you were hoping
that your grandchildren would one day inherit your
business, you presumably did not have your daughter-in-
law's children in mind.

The feelings of parents are something that you may end
up having to live with—though the pain and loss of people
whose children divorce is a feature of our society that does
not get enough recognition. There may also be a feeling
among your friends that you are doing something a bit odd,

UNDERSTANDING THE ADULTS IN STEP-FAMILIES 169

and again this is something that you may not be able to do much about (or be too bothered by). Your parents' and friends' attitude is not unimportant, because it may make for some defensiveness in your attitude to what you are embarking on, and this can be a source of strain, leading to an edginess in your life that it would be better to be without. It can also lead to the sort of determination to prove everybody wrong that we discussed in Chapter 1, which in turn may involve pretending to oneself that difficulties do not exist, instead of tackling them when they arise.

It may be necessary, then, to swallow that there may be more surprise than pleasure in the reaction to your news on the part of people who are important to you, but there may be nastier reactions than surprise. Future step-parents may pick up an assumption that they are doing their potential partners a favour, and their partners are likely to be getting a similar reaction—that they are lucky to find someone to take on the children as well as the adult. For step-parents this patronising assumption that you are doing a favour and that the biological parent is lucky to have got you will often be overlaid by the idea that you are something of a hero or heroine—and possibly somewhat foolhardy. Behind such assumptions lie others that cluster around single parents—that they are perhaps a bit morally reprehensible, or lame dogs, and therefore fortunate if they can find anyone to 'take them on'.

People can think what they wish, but if, as a step-parent or potential step-parent, you find yourself taking seriously such ideas, they need to be strenuously resisted. If you enter a relationship with the notion—however half-formed or deeply buried—that you are somehow doing the other person a favour, then this is likely to make the development of a serious relationship between adults almost impossible, because you are tacitly despising your partner. If your partner becomes aware of this—and it is hard to see how it would not be obvious in any relationship —then it will lead to a sense of worthlessness and the collapse of self-esteem.

If a step-parent has any lingering beliefs that anyone is

170   STEP-PARENTS AND THEIR CHILDREN

doing anyone else a favour, it is worth pausing for a moment over a second common whisper among family and friends—'friends' needs to be in inverted commas here—when they get the news that you are about to become a step-parent. This is the even more patronising notion that you could not find any one better. The idea is that you have failed to find a conventional single partner in the romantic stakes, so are reduced to taking second best—someone with children, in other words. This is equally offensive to both partners, but on the whole the implied criticism is of the potential step-parent who is now seen to be in need of rescue, instead of being a heroic rescuer of the unfortunate.

Such nastiness on the part of one's friends and relations may be unwelcome and unpalatable, but it could have a counterpart in an attitude that is common in step-families, and that is an imperceptible but real sense of disappointment. There is no point in pretending that a step-family is in all its details the happily-ever-after ideal that children spend their early years looking forward to. Step-families can be happy-ever-after, but it is hard to square them with the romantic model that marriages are supposed to resemble. They are a compromise, and compromises inevitably involve losing something from the ideal, which may leave a feeling that what has been achieved is only second best. When trying to make sense of their world, and make their domestic lives as satisfying as they can, people in step-families may need to acknowledge that there is an element of resentment, derived from disappointment, that can colour their perceptions of their lives.

There will be cases when the potential step-parent sees the children as a bonus, and the chance of spending time with them entirely delightful, but as often as not the children will be either irrelevant or an obstruction to the motives for becoming involved with their biological parent. Where the children are a positive calculation in the development of the new adult relationship, as against a more or less inconvenient factor in it, there may be two motives at work. The first of these is the wish on the part of the step-parent to be a rescuer. This is a common desire among children, who are prone to latch on to stray animals

UNDERSTANDING THE ADULTS IN STEP-FAMILIES   171

or to imagine themselves in heroic roles, and an impulse to rescue people in trouble is a most necessary part of social life, without which it would be difficult to provide fire services or lifeboats. It may not be a helpful motive for entering a relationship, though, since it needs a vulnerable person to succeed, and it is not healthy for children to be kept vulnerable, and since it implies a balance of power in the household that may be difficult to sustain. The children, and their parent, will sooner or later get fed up with being rescued, and resentful of being forever in the subordinate position that it implies; as for the rescuer, he or she is liable to get discouraged when any gratitude eventually wears away.

The second motive that involves the children is that of a biological parent who enters a new relationship specifically to recruit a second parent for the children. Such a motive is understandable, but it involves constricting the step-parents' individuality, so that they are not left to work out their own relationships with the children but are cast into roles that suggest they are being used for another person's purposes—and that is not to treat someone as a whole human being, but as a means to an end, and will sooner or later go wrong when the person gets tired of being used and having his or her individuality disregarded.

Setting up a step-family, then, often involves overcoming hostile gossip as well as a natural sense of disappointment for the adults. It can involve suspect motives, while the hostile environments that step-families often inhabit can hinder the development of equal relationship between the adults, and lead to an environment in which people are not seen as individuals in their own right, but as means to serving some purpose of one or other of the adults. With these unpleasant ideas out in the open, let us now turn to the two adults in the step-household, and consider their situations and what they have to contend with.

A   THE BIOLOGICAL PARENT

The Situation
On the face of it, the biological parent has the best of the

172 STEP-PARENTS AND THEIR CHILDREN

deal in a step-family—a new partner, help with caring for the children, fewer adjustments to make in relationships than either the children or the step-parent, and living with people whom he or she has chosen to be with, not had foisted upon them, like the children, nor accepted as part of a job-lot, like the step-parent. Indeed, there is a sense in which step-families might be said to exist for the main benefit of the biological parent, with fewer disadvantages than anyone else in the household.

Such a view misses the point. The biological parent is faced with different, but not necessarily easier, adjustments and tasks, and the idea of a biological parent being able to relax while the children and the step-parent struggle to come to terms with their new situation, is absurd. Biological parents in step-families have their own challenges to face, and some distinctive difficulties in tackling them. For convenience we can split these challenges into three different functions, but as always life is less tidy: the three do not follow one another in neat succession, and none of them is likely to be completed until the children have left home, and not always even then.

a *Unfinished Business*
The first task facing the biological parent is disposing of all the old unfinished business that is hanging around from the past. Relationships don't just end. Our lives are the fossil-records of past relationships, and we go on being influenced by what happened between us and another person even when that person is no longer a physical presence in our lives. Since children are prominent legacies of previous relationships, step-families contain more than usual living reminders of the past, and inevitably have to live with constant intrusions from earlier relationships and experiences. It is the biological parent who has most to do with this unfinished business. Some of it will have to do with the practical management of maintaining a child's relationship with its absent biological parent, which may involve contact with someone whom one might prefer to be at the bottom of the ocean. Even where there is no direct contact, however, the lingering presence of a previous

UNDERSTANDING THE ADULTS IN STEP-FAMILIES   173

partner in one's life may still be obtrusive. This presence is by no means always unpleasant, particularly where the partner has died, when there may be very warm memories; and even where a relationship has ended because it had become intolerable, it is still possible for it to evolve into something friendly and supportive. Lots of people who find themselves unable to live together can have a very agreeable arm's-length relationship. Generally, however, one's feelings towards the absent parent of one's children are not likely to be too cordial. You could be forgiven for thinking that you have all the inconvenience and work and worry, and that the absent parent has all the fun—making periodic glamorous outings with the children and delivering them back to you just as tiredness is starting to make them unpleasant. Such an understandable feeling is often the cause of anger, which is a common emotion among biological parents, and makes handling the unfinished business all the harder. This anger may be at one's previous partner, at things not being more straightforward, at oneself for one's failures, at the children for being there, and so on.

In the matter of unfinished business, anger can lead to the prosecution of pointless feuds, and it can get in the way of the sort of rational arrangements that may be necessary. If you are intent on making life difficult for your former partner, the children provide an obvious means—you could, for instance, try leaving it until the last moment to let the biological parent know that one of the children has chicken pox and cannot stay for the weekend after all. Sometimes the anger is directed against the children, who undoubtedly are a complication even if they are not constant reminders of someone you would prefer to forget. Sometimes it is directed at oneself, at the mistakes and misjudgements that have led one to this situation, and such anger is liable to become depression, which in turn involves low morale, and the loss of energy and pleasure.

As often as not, however, the legacy of past relationships is not simple anger, but a more mixed emotion. Our feelings towards people are seldom straightforward, and our feelings about our former and our new partner, and

174 STEP-PARENTS AND THEIR CHILDREN

about the children, are all likely to be confused. In the trade this is known as ambivalence. With the remarkable capacity of distance to lend enchantment to the view, and of nostalgia to put a skin of pleasure over the most dismal of experiences, many sane people find themselves looking back fondly at a period in their lives when they were in fact totally miserable, and populating that period with people who now do not seem too bad after all, but at the time were negligent or cruel. If a new relationship runs into a bad patch, then a previous relationship, however disastrous, may again seem attractive, and feelings begin to stir that one had assumed were dead.

Sorting out the unfinished business in the biological parent's life, then, is liable to be dogged by emotions that hinder what is in any case a difficult task. As we saw in the previous chapter, the lives of step-children are often greatly affected by loss, and the same is true of the biological parent. He or she will have experienced the self-same loss as they, and will similarly have to deal with the loss in order to rebuild a life. Anger, depression and nostalgia mix together to make strange combinations, so the unfinished business is likely to remain unfinished, and it is not usually possible to draw a line across one's life and start again.

b *Rebuilding*

The second task facing a biological parent in a step-family is to build a new life, and there is a risk that this is going to be dogged by feelings brought forward from the past. In many cases, of course, the opposite will happen. Being in love leads to a great upsurge of emotional energy, and many parents find that a previous sluggish level of emotion stemming from loneliness and depression gets replaced by a zest for life which makes it possible to offer a greater level of love to the children as well as to the new partner. There is the added advantage that replacing a lone-parent household by a step-family often does wonders for the financial security of everyone involved. In such circumstances the past can fade into unimportance, and the parent can be free to channel the new-found energy into

UNDERSTANDING THE ADULTS IN STEP-FAMILIES 175

the third task, that of maintaining the emotional fabric of the new household.

Not all step-families are started on such a wave of affection and high spirits. Many are created by a gradual process of drift, as two people find that they have unintentionally developed a level of involvement, and the future has become taken for granted almost before the people involved have realised that it exists. Other step-families are created after a cautious assessment of the possible balance sheet of profit and loss, with no high expectations or hopes, but simply from an unexcited calculation that the people involved would be better off emotionally and financially if they set up house together. Incorporated into this calculation will most likely be a determination not to be hurt by disappointed expectations or unreal commitments.

Whatever the degree of exuberance with which the step-family was established, however, the spectre of the past is likely to have put in an appearance, however decorous, at the feast, and most biological parents are going to have to take some account of their feelings about the past as they embark on their new life. Where there was a period of lone-parenthood before the step-family was established, the immediate strength of feelings associated with the end of the previous relationship may have faded, and where there has been a prolonged period of lone-parenthood, some sort of accommodation of these complex feelings will almost always have been achieved—not necessarily a satisfactory one, nor one that does justice to the complexity of feeling, but a manageable arrangement nevertheless. When a new partner enters the situation, this arrangement is going to be disturbed. A whole new package of domestic and emotional agreements has to be negotiated. And so it happens that at a time when biological parents are supposed to be happy, they find themselves feeling wretched.

There are two causes of this wretchedness. One is the difficulty of the situation, for setting up a step-family is hard and stressful. The second has to do with intrusions from the past. Often, when a relationship comes to an end, the adult who is caring for the children is too frantically busy to have time to mourn the loss, and only too aware of the need to remain 'strong' and not give way to the anger and grief that are to be found on these occasions (even when the dominant emotion is relief). With the installation of a step-parent, the paramount need to ward off disabling emotions may be less, and in consequence some biological parents find themselves in sadness at the ending of the old relationship when they should be feeling happy because of the new one. A related process is that the new relationship reminds people of the hopes and happiness that may have been around at the outset of the old one, and so will bring to mind all the disappointment at what happened to all the hope and happiness.

c *Emotional Juggling*

The third task facing a biological parent is to keep the emotional life of the household in shape. This is not an unshared responsibility, but the bulk of it probably falls on the biological parent unless the step-parent is also bringing children into the new household. It is a long-term task, and at its simplest may be described as a case of balancing conflicting and competing demands. As with so much of what concerns us in this book, describing it is the easiest thing about it.

Children, in the nature of things, will continue to make demands whatever the details of their domestic environment. In the early years of a step-family's life, the children will look to their biological parent for the bulk of these needs, and their demands are likely to be increased if the children perceive any threat to themselves in the new situation. On top of the children's demands will be those of the new partner who will be looking for an independent and private share of time, attention and love. The life of the biological parent in all this is one of wrenchingly divided loyalties—divided between the claims of children and the new partner and perhaps other people, such as his or her own parents, as well as the claims of one's own needs and wishes.

The biological parent, in short, is likely to feel tugged in

UNDERSTANDING THE ADULTS IN STEP-FAMILIES 177

all directions at once—and this at a time when he or she is supposed to be happy. When the relationship is new, it is supposed to replicate the bliss of the first engagement and marriage. For women who have never had a stable relationship with the father or fathers of their children, this new relationship is supposed to incorporate them into the conventional world and to signal that their troubles can now be forgotten in the rapture of the new situation. All perfectly true, no doubt, but failing to notice the worm that life has a habit of leaving around in the choicest of buds.

When there is a discrepancy between what you are feeling and what you are supposed to feel, or think you should be feeling, you are liable to become demoralised and unhappy. The strain of putting a cheerful face on things compounds the strain that is already there, and where all this is topped up with a lavish amount of guilt at not being a 'good' parent, and at not meeting in full all the new partner's expectations, and at having brought about the children's predicament, then it is hardly surprising that the past looks so attractive in its simplicity. So when people assume, as many do, that step-families exist largely for the benefit of the biological parent, the biological parents in question may be forgiven a hollow laugh.

The majority of biological parents living in step-families are women, and women in western societies are especially prone to depression. The most likely response to the strains of managing the emotional life of a step-family is, therefore, a depressed biological parent, overwhelmed by the pressures of the situation. Some parents, however, will protect themselves by looking for a convenient scapegoat. Scapegoating has been discussed in Chapter 5, so now we need only observe that the most obvious people to blame are the children, without whom none of this would be happening. When this happens, the risk is that the children, who may be uncertain enough of their place in the new household and in the parent's affections, are liable to feel squeezed out, replaced by the new parent, and the object of their biological parent's anger. When children feel like this, they are liable to behave 'badly' as we saw in

178   STEP-PARENTS AND THEIR CHILDREN

Chapter 4, as they enact their anger in retaliation against the world, or as they test the quality of their parent's love.

Survival Strategies for Biological Parents

The biological parent, then, has to perform difficult emotional and practical tasks in the present with the additional handicap of emotional freight from the past to make things harder. There are five strategies to make things easier—though never, unfortunately, easy.

a   Clean out the Emotional Attic

The first is to do what you can to clear out the lumber from the past. You will never dispose of it completely, and it is not right that you should, for what happened was real, however we may regret the consequences. But we can cut down on the burden of guilt by subjecting our guilt to the sort of rational interrogation that we discussed in Chapter 1. Ask yourself what exactly was so wrong in your behaviour, and whether it offended against your own worked-out moral standards, as against the half-considered prejudices that we carry forward into adult life from our childhood. We can also stop fighting battles that were lost long since, and in particular we can abandon old feuds, and make an effort to stop regretting what cannot be changed.

b   Cultivate Self-Knowledge

All the above implies a high level of honesty about one's feelings, and trying to cultivate this honesty is the second thing that a biological parent can do to make life easier. Acknowledging to oneself that one's feelings towards the children or a new partner are not straightforward, but often comprise negative things like resentment embedded in the positive things like love, is not easy. It involves admitting things about oneself that most of us would prefer not to recognise or acknowledge, but the alternative is to maintain a self-image that sooner or later will involve lying to oneself, and lying again to hide the lie, and this will lead to a frustrating round of increasingly desperate self-deception that will require an ever-growing amount of emotional energy to feed—energy that will have to be

UNDERSTANDING THE ADULTS IN STEP-FAMILIES 179

withdrawn from areas of life in which it could be more
beneficially used, like caring for one's children. Honesty
does not mean shouting things from the housetops, but it
promises at least a partial release from this round of self-
deception and the strain associated with it.

c *Share Your Feelings*
The third thing to do is to find someone to share your
feelings with. The obvious person is your partner, a
natural source of support and encouragement. He or she
will be having problems, too, and these may bear a striking
resemblance to what you are experiencing. The euphoria
that step-parents might be hoping for may be looking a bit
tatty if they cannot get into the bathroom which is
permanently occupied by their new step-children, and, like
biological parents, step-parents may be finding that their
joy is not thriving in uncomplicated isolation; they, too, are
disturbed by the discrepancy between what they think, or
indeed know, that they should be feeling, and what they
actually are. You may not feel that you want to add to all
this, but perhaps your partner is also reluctant to intrude
on your supposed unalloyed contentment with the news
that he or she is not having much fun. The recognition
that you are both experiencing something similar would be
a useful starting point to doing something about it, as well
as enriching at least one aspect of your lives, your
relationship with one another.

Instead of, or as well as, your partner, it may be helpful to
try to find other people in the same boat. You may not be
able to find a friend you can trust not to gossip, and many
people in any case find it an enormous relief to discover
that they are not alone in what they had supposed was a
uniquely difficult or embarrassing situation. One of the
purposes of this book is to make clear that there are plenty
of other people who are going through similar experiences,
but it is usually better to meet such people rather than to be
made aware of them through a book. You are likely to meet
people with similar problems by seeking out a step-parents'
group, or joining any similar group that intends to offer its
members support with the problems of their daily lives.

180   STEP-PARENTS AND THEIR CHILDREN

Since a major problem for a biological parent who is being torn apart by the competing demands of members of the household is isolation, finding a group can be very helpful with this aspect of the problem.

d   *Develop a Routine to Cut Down Stress*
The fourth way in which biological parents can ease their lives is by devising a routine to minimise stress. Again we come back to the notion of the family as a machine for living in, and the importance of looking for mechanical ways of making it run better. In practical terms, this involves negotiating and setting aside separate time and space for your children and for your partner. Doing this requires important concessions: it means acknowledging that the step-family is often (or usually) less of a place of intimate unity than are most biological families, and that step-families have their own histories that it may not be comfortable to remember and admit, but will not go away. You will not be able to make sure that the children have their own time, and by this means cut down on the competition, if you insist that everything has to be done as a group, that the adults are an indissoluble couple, not two individuals, and that children are not permitted an individual relationship with individual parents. Some biological families live like this, and it seems to work, although most probably accept that family relationships are never completely balanced and that a particular child and a particular parent will often have a private arrangement that undermines parental unity and could be called favouritism.

Step-families comprise relationships with different histories. The children's relationship with their biological parent is older than their relationship with their step-parent, and older, too, than the relationship between the two adults (at least in its present form—obviously the adults may have known each other for years before they set up house). So pretending that the adults have no private relationships with the children runs against common sense and against what the children know to be the case, and it also ignores a crucial fact about families, which is that they evolve organically, and do not come into

UNDERSTANDING THE ADULTS IN STEP-FAMILIES 181

existence by a one-off act. The arrival of a step-parent in the household changes things, obviously, but it does not create a family in the sense that the term usually means. If you insist that the family functions only as a group, you may seem to be repudiating the relationship between the biological parent and the children, and if you require that the children from now on relate to two adults, one of whom is possibly something of a stranger, then you are doing violence to that relationship, and can expect trouble and resentment.

e *Welcome Change*
If we accept that families evolve organically, then they must be *allowed* to evolve, which means creating the atmosphere in which change can happen, and not trying to cling to original relationships in an unchanged form. To pretend that nothing has changed when a step-parent comes on the scene is just as silly as pretending that everything has. Your feelings towards the children may not have changed—indeed, they may have improved if you have more emotional energy now that you are less lonely and depressed—but the form and the circumstances have changed and the relationship has to change its quality accordingly. Wanting things to be just as they always were is a common enough human feeling, but unfortunately time goes on its indifferent way and things change as it passes, so clinging to the form of relationship that existed before the step-parent arrived is impossible since it would have changed anyway. Where there is guilt and uncertainty, it may be tempting to try to cling to old intimacies without accepting that they would certainly alter, but they need to change if they are to live.

The biological parent in a step-family is much less fortunate than some people suppose. Far from basking in untroubled ease, while the rest of the household sort out their relationships with one another, the biological parent has distinctive tasks, and an unpromising atmosphere in which to carry them out. There are ways of making life easier, but the problems will almost certainly survive in one form or another.

182 STEP-PARENTS AND THEIR CHILDREN

B THE STEP-PARENT

Since this whole book is aimed mainly at step-parents, this section can afford to be brief, and all I shall do is identify some broad features of a step-parent's situation, and show how they might affect domestic life. Earlier in this chapter, we talked about some of the things that get said—or thought—when someone becomes a step-parent, and also suggested that step-parents would do well to think twice if they hoped to rescue people, or otherwise felt sorry for the members of their new household. I suggested that there is often an element of disappointment in becoming a step-parent, and that the negative feelings that a step-parent may have need acknowledging if one is to do the job conscientiously.

Some Common Pitfalls

If it is not most people's first choice to become a step-parent, and if becoming one may involve putting up with some surprise, even disbelief, from other people in your life, but if, nevertheless, you decide to go ahead, there are four basic approaches that need to be avoided. Three of these stem, at least in part, from an attempt to make up for the loss of an ideal: they are to use the children as a means to an end in the relationship, to try to exclude them as far as possible, and to go for an 'instant family' model of one's domestic life. All these involve depriving the children of their own importance and individuality, and are therefore against the children's interests, and usually self-defeating ways of approaching step-parenting. The fourth approach involves the step-parent failing to find any real place in the family's life.

a *Using Children as Go-Betweens*

First, using the children as a means to an end in relating with the adult. Your potential partner and his or her children are at once a collection of individuals and a unit. They are a unit in the sense that you get them all or none of them, and that they have a relationship that is held together by bonds that were developed before you came on the scene and owe their strength to past experiences and the loyalties that

UNDERSTANDING THE ADULTS IN STEP-FAMILIES 183

have come from these experiences. If, as is usual but not invariable, your interest in this unit is heavily skewed towards one member of it—the adult, your potential partner—then it might be understandable if you try to employ the subordinate members of the unit to foster your relationship with the important member. Put like that, it may seem that we are describing pretty crude manipulation, but it is common enough for this process to happen almost innocently and certainly without any attempt at guile. For instance, bringing a present for a child is in itself a harmless and attractive thing for an adult to do. The problem arises when the main purpose of bringing the present is wanting to look attractive, to signal to the child's parent that you are a caring and worthwhile person who should be looked upon favourably. There is no way out of this dilemma, because one does not give presents to children with whom one has no involvement, and the involvement that authorises the giving of presents, or otherwise taking an interest, stems from your relationship with the parent. The thing to avoid is using the children as a means of ingratiating yourself with their parent, and to lose sight of their claims on your time and thought as individuals in their own right, and as people with whom you are considering becoming deeply involved. A lot of step-children feel very conscious —correctly—that their step-parent regards them as merely an appendage to their parent, who is the real object of the step-parent's interest. It needs a lot of care and thought to prevent this preference from becoming translated into ignoring the children's individuality and importance as autonomous individuals. Allowing an interest to develop that focuses on the children as independent beings may take considerable effort.

b *Excluding the Children*
The second way of misusing the children is to try to exclude them from the relationship. In extreme cases, there are step-parents who ignore the children, managing never to speak to them or to take any interest in them. Such extremes are rare, but not unknown. Much more common is a subtler but systematic elbowing of the

184   STEP-PARENTS AND THEIR CHILDREN

children out of the real relationship in the household. Human beings are very good at developing special relationships within a group: we learn to do it as children when we strive to establish private relationships with one or another parent or with a particular brother or sister, and at school we acquire considerable skills in carving out special friendships within a group of less important ones. Superficially the group is intact. It goes around together as a unit, whether a family unit or a school group, but the pairings within that group are fully understood, and the special friendships are recognised, especially by those who would like to break them up. When we get older we behave more correctly, avoiding arguments about who is going to sit next to whom on the school bus, though our children may still engage in that sort of rivalry, and parents in even the most orderly households will have to keep this sort of thing in check. Potential and actual step-children, because they are young, will, therefore, be fully immersed in the world of competition for friendship, and may be highly sophisticated in reading the signs, and aware of any attempts to cut them out. So though the step-parent's strategies to marginalise the children may be subtle and polite enough, falling well short of the strategy of ignoring them, to the children they may be brutally clear.

If the step-parent is determined not to push the children out, and to treat them as individuals who have as much right to the biological parent's time and affection as the step-parent has, then it may not be enough to accept gracefully when you are outmanoeuvred by highly-skilled and sophisticated operators in the matter of who sits where on a train or in front of the television: it may be necessary to remind oneself that there nestles a child, with a child's needs and skills, within even the most grown-up of us, and that this child within the step-parent may be trying to exclude the real children from their relationship with their own parent. Unless we recognise our own childish streak, there is a danger that we could be unaware of what we are doing; in that case, the child within the step-parent could become a menace to the future of the household.

UNDERSTANDING THE ADULTS IN STEP-FAMILIES   185

c   *Creating Spurious Families*

The third danger is one that we have mentioned periodically throughout this book. It is trying to bash the domestic unit into an 'instant family', looking as much like the 'ideal' nuclear family as possible, ignoring its distinctive history and trying to create the sort of unity and closeness that 'real' families are supposed to have. The children are expected to rethink their lives, to forget much of what has happened, to reject the form of relationship in the immediate past, and to accept this newcomer as their parent in all that the word implies. The process is not usually as abrupt as this, of course, but the temptation is for some people to try to put together as close a resemblance as possible to the ideal family as a way of hiding their disappointment that they have arrived at a household that is not what they had been brought up to expect. There may be a hasty change of name, the development of a regime that allows nobody in the household any time or opportunity for private relationships, where leisure is spent in a rather hectic effort to demonstrate to the world what a close-knit and happy set-up this is. It may involve an excessive punctiliousness at parents' evenings at school, an over-enthusiastic involvement in what it is assumed parents engage in, all to silence the still, small voice that whispers that this is not a real family, not what you looked forward to, not what you saw yourself as part of, not what you imagined that your future would hold.

d   *Staying Outside*

All these pitfalls are common and understandable enough, but they involve a heavy-handed treatment of the domestic life that existed before the step-parent came along. This life was a subtle and complex web of relationships. It brought together loyalties and rivalries, love and jealousy, compromise, rules and conventions, decisions about the extent of people's privacy, about what things are to be shared and what are not to be shared—and all the rest of the numberless details of a group of people trying to live together. With the arrival of a step-parent, there are bound

186 STEP-PARENTS AND THEIR CHILDREN

to be major, perhaps monumental, changes, but the inevitability of change does not justify anyone in failing to respect the richness and complexity of this domestic life. It is the location of many of the most important things in people's lives, and it is wrong to devalue it even though it is bound to change. Trying to extract one member of this group for one's private needs, to value some members only because of the access that they give you to another member, or to redefine the whole package of relationships and traditions because you are disappointed at your situation, is not only insensitive and crass, but extremely foolish. It is bound to cause resentment, discomfort, and, at the worst, retaliation as the incumbents combine together to expel the intruder.

A peaceful and welcoming absorption of a step-parent into an existing domestic arrangement is only going to happen if the step-parent values the importance of the existing household, and respects the relationships that it embodies and people's stake in it. In doing this, though, a step-parent has to guard against the fourth risk, that of never losing the sense of being an intruder with no right to be there, a mute onlooker in the affairs of the household, a temporary visitor forever apologising for one's presence, embarrassed at being there when the private business of the family is worked out. As well as being uncomfortable, such an attitude is also unrealistic, for the household cannot remain unaffected by a newcomer, and if its members try to preserve unchanged the arrangement that they had before the step-parent arrived, they are doing something that is as ill-judged as some of the things that step-parents might do, and as insensitive to the legitimate claims of the step-parent as some step-parents are to the claims of the existing household. To the extent that the people trying to preserve the *status quo* and to keep the newcomer as much as possible on the sidelines are children, then the attempt is both more understandable and more forgivable. Certainly, the step-parent should try not to tread on people's feelings, and may have a desperate wish to avoid confrontation; but he or she needs also to keep firmly in mind that he or she has a perfect right to be there, and should resolve not to be intimidated. This right to be there has to be asserted with tact. You do not go unasked into the children's bedrooms or use their things, even though many biological parents treat their children's privacy with scant respect, and you recognise that there are certain aspects of the children's lives that are more your business than others; but there is a workable balance between bad-mannered assertion and inappropriate apology that can be negotiated by people who have thought the matter through.

The Power of Time
Very often, the longer a step-family lasts, the more manageable its problems become. The reasons for this are not difficult to suggest—that patterns of life evolve as the children get older and their needs and expectations, as well as their means of coping with their domestic life, change. In the process of change the newcomer becomes adapted into the system. Where initial fears and insecurities are without real foundation, and the adults are committed to preserving a safe and stable home for the children, then time will allow children to become convinced of the goodwill within the new household, and the adults will have a chance to lay to rest their own anxieties and the sort of feelings of insecurity that make them tense and quarrelsome. If this is true, it is all the wiser for a new step-parent to be patient, to allow the situation to evolve and to give time for the process of absorption. Patience will get better results than trying to squeeze the household into conformity with a private blueprint, or to muscle into a role that one feels one should adopt within the household. A little humility, a prudent hesitancy, and an awareness that for many people change is deeply menacing, and that the life of the household before you arrived had a value to its members even though they were deprived of the privilege of your presence, will lead to a courteous patience. It will let your absorption happen gradually, at a pace that is comfortable for the existing members of the family, and which will allow your personality and needs, and those of the existing members, to enmesh harmoniously and pleasurably.

SECTION IV

PRACTICAL INFORMATION

8 LEGAL ASPECTS OF STEP-PARENTING

Many step-families are never going to be troubled by the legal aspects of their situation. Some families are not so fortunate, however, and endure years of misery and uncertainty as their personal relationships are hacked about in the gladiatorial world of the courts. The crucial legal decision affecting most step-families is the one about custody of the children, and this will usually have been made before the step-family comes into being. There are, however, a number of situations in which step-parenting may involve legal difficulties, and this chapter aims to identify these. The word 'identify' needs emphasising, because if a step-family encounters any of the problems, the adults would do well to seek qualified legal advice, and should certainly *not* rely on the information in this chapter, which relates only to England and Wales, and may well be out of date by the time you read it. It is also necessary to make clear that I take the view that it is the questions of personal relationships that are important in these matters, not the narrowly legalistic aspects: so, for instance, the question of whether you adopt your step-children, or change their names, may ultimately be decided by a court, but the decision to apply to the court needs to follow careful thought about the human implications of the question.

With these preliminary cautions, it is possible to identify a number of situations in which legal complications might arise.

1 The Custody of Children

Where the step-children are the children of divorce, the Divorce Court will have decided which parent should have custody of them, and may have laid down conditions to this custody. If the step-parent is living in the household at the

192 STEP-PARENTS AND THEIR CHILDREN

time of the divorce, or is about to do so, then the court will consider this in deciding the question of custody. Things may be different if a step-parent comes along later, because the original decision about custody was made on the basis of the parents' lives as they were at the time of the court case. If the circumstances of the parent who has custody changes by developing a relationship with a new partner, then it might be that the court would want to look again. The welfare of the child is the paramount concern, and if the potential step-parent is thought to be unsuitable in some way, then the custody arrangements could be changed. It is certainly not the case, however, that courts are interested in every potential step-parent, and when the matter of custody is re-opened at the time when a step-family is being formed, it is often because there was a dispute over custody at the time of the divorce, and the unsuccessful parent wants the matter re-opened because he or she has not accepted the fairness or rightness of the original decision. Obviously courts are not going to upset a working arrangement where they feel that the main issue is the continuing feud between the parents, and as many non-custodial parents quickly lose significant contact with the children, it follows that the majority of potential step-parents have nothing to worry about as far as the courts are concerned. At a human level, it seems to me to be obviously right to make a non-custodial parent aware of the situation when a step-parent is moving into the household, because such a move is important for the children, and the non-custodial parent is entitled to know what is happening in the life of his or her children. Some non-custodial parents try to veto the proposed arrangement by recourse to law, but it is rare for them to succeed. Where the custodial parent 'won' custody in a disputed divorce, then it would be especially sensible to seek advice.

2 Adoption
There was a time when step-parents commonly adopted the children. This made the step-parent a parent in all the legal senses of the term: it effectively deprived the non-custodial parent of any involvement with the child,

LEGAL ASPECTS OF SELF-PARENTING 193

automatically changed the child's name—and was irrevocable. Adoption by step-parents has become much less common, and there is now available a sort of mid-way position, custodianship. The custodian (a singularly unfortunate choice of word, raising images of jailors with keys) has full responsibility for the children, in the sense of being able to make decisions about them and on their behalf. This regularises the step-parent's relationship with the children, and so removes some of the insecurity that may be implicit in the step-parental situation. This insecurity can range from matters like signing certain documents at school, to an ambiguity about the step-parent's claims to continue to care for a child should the partner die. Unlike adoption, a custodianship order is not irrevocable, and it does not exclude the non-custodial parent from contact with the children. The child retains its rights of inheritance and nationality. Throughout this book, I have argued that it is often a mistake to try to push a step-family into a close resemblance to a biological family, and if it seems right to preserve a sense of the 'stepness' of the household, custodianship rather than adoption will often fit its psychological needs. It is therefore unfortunate that these orders are not available to the majority of step-parents, since children who have been subject to the jurisdiction of a divorce court are not normally eligible.

There is much anguish experienced in households where a non-custodial parent is forever trying to regain the custody of the children, but in such cases the non-custodial parent's consent will often be needed for an adoption, and will presumably not usually be forthcoming. We have discussed in this book some of the problems associated with a non-custodial parent having access to the children, and noticed the distinctive flavour that such matters impart to step-family life. To try to resolve such difficulties has been a common motive for adopting children, but courts will now rightly give short shrift to applications to adopt that appear to be based on such motives, and are increasingly recognising that contact between children and their non-custodial parent is a right that the *children* have, as much as—or more than—the parent. In certain circum-

194 STEP-PARENTS AND THEIR CHILDREN

stances, courts must make a custodianship order, rather than an adoption order, and it seems likely that adoptions by step-parents will continue to decline.

This wish to adopt is a perfectly understandable one, however, and in many cases will continue to be entirely appropriate. Examples of these would be a child whose father is unknown, or a child who is 'illegitimate' (hardly a serious stigma in this day and age, one would like to think, but, alas, one that still seems to survive). Some older children may wish to be adopted, because that would confirm a commitment and level of involvement that might be very important to them. In all such cases, however, it would be important to balance the costs against the benefits. A legal order that abolishes the claims of a biological parent may also effectively abolish the involvement of grandparents and other members of the child's extended family, which could be sad for everyone concerned.

3 Names

The consent of a child's non-custodial parent is necessary if the child's surname is to be changed, unless the custodial parent has sole parental rights. A court may over-rule the biological parent's objection, but to repeat the general drift of the argument in Chapter 3, names carry important emotional connotations, and people should think carefully before changing them.

4 The Break-Up of a Step-Family

Step-children are children of the family, so courts *can* make an order giving a step-parent custody or access should the step-family split up. By the same token, a step-parent can be ordered to make a financial contribution to the support of his or her step-children.

The death of the biological parent is likely to have catastrophic consequences unless that parent has made a will appointing the step-parent guardian to the children. Without such a will, a step-parent has no necessary right to continue to care for the children, and at the very least could face a legal wrangle in the midst of a bereavement. If you would wish and expect to have the care of your step-children should your partner die, then it is imperative that you persuade him or her to make a will.

5 Inheritance

In order to minimise any future unpleasantness, it is probably more important for step-parents than for biological parents to make a will. Where a step-parent dies without making a will, a step-child is not excluded from a share in the estate, but because there are often other possible beneficiaries, in the shape of previous spouses and children from other marriages, the potential for a lawyers' beanfeast is obvious. The emotional aspects of making a will are discussed in Chapter 3. The practicalities are not for amateurs, so step-parents should not be tempted to buy a form from a stationer's shop and attempt to make their own will. Such a will may be perfectly legal, but may not embody your intentions in unequivocal terms; in view of the complexity of many step-families' circumstances, getting professional help is advisable.

6 Parental Rights and Responsibilities

Step-parents have few automatic rights over the children (which seems to me on the whole a desirable state of affairs, since children are not items of property), but they do have obligations. The law in this area is highly ambiguous, but the position of step-parents is undoubtedly a weak one. They have no power to decide matters such as a step-child's religion, or how it should be educated, but they may be held responsible for its financial support. Their right to discipline a child is only because they are acting on behalf of the biological parent—when their position seems to be roughly that of a school-teacher. Step-parents have to care for children in an acceptable manner, and they can be held responsible for their step-children's behaviour (by having to pay fines imposed by courts, for instance). The law seems to recognise only step-parents who are married to a child's biological parent, so if you are living together without having formalised your relationship by marriage, then your position may in certain circumstances be very precarious.

196 STEP-PARENTS AND THEIR CHILDREN

7 Miscellaneous

Step-parents may not theoretically be able to sign forms
agreeing to medical treatment, or write notes explaining a
child's absence from school, or allowing it to go on a school
trip, but in practice there are few difficulties in this area. A
child cannot be on a step-parent's passport unless it is
adopted, so it will need a separate passport to travel with
the step-parent but without the biological parent. There
may be restrictions on travel if the child's custody has been
decided by a court, and the non-custodial parent may be
able to object to its travel, particularly if it is proposed to
leave the country.

9 SOURCES OF HELP

Many step-parents are so anxious to resist the common image of 'wickedness' that they put a determinedly optimistic front on their lives which may stop them from seeking help when they first need it. As a result, matters that could perhaps have been fairly easily sorted out are allowed to fester, and by the time people get round to seeking help, family relationships may have become unnecessarily poisoned. It makes sense, therefore, to look for help sooner rather than later. There are a number of sources of help available.

Informal Help
For many step-parents, the most helpful people are other step-parents. Your circumstances will never be identical, but with other step-parents you can be sure of finding someone who will not be disposed to criticise too readily, and who will have experiences that are comparable with yours and which may be useful to you. The chances are that you already know other step-parents. If you do, the problem may be to alter your relationship from a purely social one to one in which it is possible to discuss common concerns, and it may be necessary to suggest to friends that you would find it helpful to meet in a formal way from time to time to compare notes on step-parenting—and not to get sidetracked into talking about the weather or work, which you can go on doing in your purely social contacts.

Many people find regular meetings of step-parents helpful. There may well be a group meeting in your area already, and you should be able to get information from your Public Library or from the local Social Services department (both of whose addresses will be in the telephone directory), or from the National Step-Family

198 STEP-PARENTS AND THEIR CHILDREN

Association (about which there is more information in the next section). If there is no group already in existence, you may want to consider starting one. An advertisement in the local newspaper will probably be answered by more than enough families to get started, and I would offer only two cautions. The first is that it is often better for such groups to meet in a public room such as can usually be hired in libraries or schools or (more expensively) from hotels, rather than in someone's private house. This is because the family whose house it is have their position rather distorted by being in some sense the host, which may inhibit free discussion, allow pointless issues of power to creep in, and make the whole experience less helpful than it might be. The second caution is that such groups often become very exciting very quickly, which tempts people to want to meet frequently. As the group gets established, however, it tends to become less exciting (though often more helpful), and people find that they have committed themselves to more than they wish to keep up. It is sensible to arrange regular meetings—perhaps monthly—that will not become a burden.

Formal Help

There are a number of organisations that will be able to help with the problems of step-parenting, or put you in touch with someone who can.

Legal and Financial Problems

You may have a solicitor who deals with your affairs and whose judgement you trust, and if you can afford it, this would be the obvious place to go to first. Solicitors are expensive, however, and you may find good specialist advice available free from a Citizens' Advice Bureau, Law Centre or Advice Centre. Such organisations are often more familiar than general solicitors with complicated but specialised areas of law such as housing and social security, and usually have professional lawyers on their staffs or available for consultation. If you cannot find a suitable source of advice through the telephone directory, your Public Library should be able to help you track one down.

SOURCES OF HELP 199

Stepfamily (The National Step-Family Association), Maris House, Maris Lane, Trumpington, Cambridge (Telephone 0223 841306) is an experienced organisation able to help with practical problems—and indeed all problems—of step-parenting.

Emotional Problems
There is no hard and fast distinction between emotional and practical problems. Difficulties that are primarily those of relationship have a habit of becoming focused in practical matters, so that people will put all the difficulties down to the house they live in—only to find that they take their problems with them when they move. It may be, therefore, that your legal and practical difficulties have been sorted out but you find that things are still not well. There are several sources of help available.

a *Stepfamily* (whose address is given in the previous section).

b *Probation Officers*. These are not just concerned with delinquents; many are very experienced in dealing with difficulties in marriages and in personal relationships in general.

c *Social Workers*. Most social workers are employed by Local Authority Social Service Departments, and are trained to help families with all aspects of their lives. They are often extremely busy, however, and many offices cannot take on all the work that they are asked to do; but they will certainly be able to suggest places to go for help if they cannot work with you themselves.

d *Marriage Guidance Councils*. These are able to help with all aspects of family relationships, not just marriage.

e *Conciliation Services*. These are available in some towns, primarily to sort out questions of access and the like, at the time of marital breakdown.

f *Specialist Agencies*. There are a number of organisations, such as Family Service Units and the NSPCC, that may be available in your area to help with difficulties in personal

200 STEP-PARENTS AND THEIR CHILDREN

relationships. There are counselling services that are independent of statutory control, and which do not necessarily charge a fee for their services—though some may. There are private psychotherapists and counsellors, many operating a sliding scale to set their fees according to your income.

g   *Child Guidance Clinics*. Most of these now adopt a family therapy approach, which involves working with the whole family, rather than with the children alone.

10 SUGGESTIONS FOR FURTHER READING

1 Research About Step-Families

A useful summary of the research evidence about how 'well' step-families function is:

Lawrence H. Ganong and Marilyn Carter, 'The effects of remarriage on children: a review of the empirical literature', *Family Relations*, Volume 33, pp. 389–506, 1984.

This paper summarises and criticises most of the work up to the time it was written—though, of course, research continues, and more has since appeared. The authors conclude, 'In general, there was little evidence that children in stepfamilies differ from children in other family structures . . .' Similar conclusions are reached, though rather more tentatively, by:

Elsa Ferri, *Stepchildren: a National Study*, NFER-Nelson, London, 1984.

This study is based on following the progress of all children born in Britain in a particular week in 1958.

2 Books for Step-Parents

The last few years has seen a steady trickle of books aimed at helping step-parents do the job better. A few of these that seem to me particularly useful are:

Elizabeth Hodder, *The Step-Parents' Handbook*, Sphere Books Ltd, London, 1985.

This is a readable and eminently practical discussion of some of the most common problems that step-parents meet. The author is the founder of the Step-Family Association, and well placed to know the problems that step-parents encounter.

Fredrick Capaldi and Barbara McRae, *Stepfamilies: a*

202   STEP-PARENTS AND THEIR CHILDREN

Cooperative Responsibility, New Viewpoints/Vision Books, New York, 1979.

The emphasis in this book is more on the psychology of step-families than the previous book, so they complement each other usefully.

Janet S. Stenson, *Now I Have a Step-Parent, and It's Kind of Confusing*, Avon, New York, 1979.

Despite its title, this contains a great deal of interest both for step-parents and for the young people towards whom it is primarily aimed.

3   Other Material

Three books that are not primarily aimed at step-parents, but which contain a lot of food for thought, are:

Emily B. Visher and John S. Visher, *Stepfamilies: A Guide to Working with Stepparents and Stepchildren*, Brunner/Mazel, New York, 1979.

This is a book intended for professionals who are involved with step-families, but provides a sophisticated general account of step-families and their situation.

Peter Laslett, *Family and Illicit Love in Earlier Generations*, Cambridge University Press, Cambridge, 1977.

This book pulls a corner of the curtain to allow a glimpse of the history of step-parenting, and will fascinate readers who are interested in the past.

Jacqueline Burgoyne and David Clark, *Making a Go of it: a Study of Stepfamilies in Sheffield*, Routledge and Kegan Paul, London, 1984.

Particularly interesting for the extensive quotations from interviews with step-families, so that we can hear the voice of real people describing their lives.

J. M. Ellis, *One Fairy Story Too Many: The Brothers Grimm and their Tales*, Chicago University Press, Chicago, 1983.

Although any rehabilitation of the wicked step-parent is subsidiary to the author's purpose, which is to evaluate the status as folklorists of the Brothers Grimm, this book shows how far the wicked step-parent was an invention of the Grimms, developed for their own purposes, and often not found in the original folk material that they claimed to be recording.

4 General Reading

Academic or theoretical books can say a lot of useful things about step-parenting, but they cannot hope to catch its richness, and for this we need to turn to the work of novelists rather than psychologists. Relationships within step-families are the central theme of two outstanding novels:

Henry James, *What Maisie Knew*, first published in 1897, and regularly reprinted;

and

Elizabeth Gaskell, *Wives and Daughters*, first published in 1866.

Both are works of extraordinary subtlety and power, and can add a depth of understanding to step-parenting that is not available from other sources. I should add a note of caution, however: neither is a book to be casually read on the beach or on a train, for they both require considerable concentration (particularly *Maisie*) if the full range of what they have to say is to be appreciated.

Finally, there is:

Edmund Gosse, *Father and Son*, first published in 1907.

An autobiography that is at once very funny and very moving. Its central theme is the relationship between Gosse and his father, but it contains an extensive account of how the life of a small boy in Victorian England was made immeasurably happier by the arrival of a step-mother.

5 Legal References

To repeat the point made in Chapter 8, if your legal circumstances are complicated, seek professional help. The old joke that the man who represents himself in court has a fool for a client is no doubt one much favoured by lawyers, but in an area as complicated as domestic law, making a mistake could be catastrophic for a lot of people. Two books make the legal position more or less intelligible for non-specialists:

Brenda M. Hoggett and David S. Pearl, *The Family, Law and Society*, Butterworths, London, 1983.

and

204 STEP-PARENTS AND THEIR CHILDREN

Brenda M. Hoggett, *Parents and Children*, Sweet and Maxwell, London, 1981.

The latter is by far the simpler, and neither is completely up to date even at the time I am writing, but they identify the main issues well enough. An admirably clear account of the law is to be found in the book by Elizabeth Hodder mentioned under 'Books for Step-Parents'.

INDEX

Note: the following conventions are used in this index:

'Absent Parent' means a biological parent not living with the children.

'Biological Parent' means a biological parent who is living with the children—in other words, the step-parent's partner.

absent parent,
  competition with, 63, 80–4, 149–50,
    159–60
  feelings of, 77–8, 88
  as scapegoat, 137
  see also access
access, 79–84
  competitiveness involved, 80–1, 84
  financial aspects, 82
  guilt, 81
  stresses of, 80–4
admiration, children's need for, 57–8
adoption, 192–4
adults, needs of, 48
affection, *see* care, jealousy, love, sex
amalgamated families, 11, 67, 123
anger, 39, 46–7, 99–101, 107
assumptions of this book, 14–15
attention-seeking, *see* 'bad behaviour'
authority, 93–101, 112 *see also* power
autobiography, 203

'bad behaviour', 101–6
  attention-seeking, 104
  defining, 101–3
  expressing unhappiness, 105–6
  inexperience, 103–4
  reasons for, 103–6
behaviour, bad, *see* 'bad behaviour'
behaviour, good, *see* 'good behaviour'
benefits of step-families, 15–16, 30–4,
  37, 70–1
biological families and step families, *see*
  differences
biological parent, 171–81

and change, 180
and depression, 177
divided loyalties, 176–8
emotional juggling, 176–8
intrusions from past, 172–4
mixed emotions, 177–9
as monitor of domestic life, 121,
  132
and new life, 174–6
and routine, 180–1
self-knowledge, 178–9
stresses on, 172–8
survival strategies, 179–81
tasks, 172–8
and unfinished business, 172–4
Bond, James, 9
books about step-parenting, 201–2
blood relationships, *see* kinship
Bunny, Bugs, 9

care, 20–1, 31–3, 58–63, 88
children,
  as go-betweens, 182–3
  custody of, *see* custody
  excluded by adults, 183–4
communicating with children, 63
comparisons, odious, 39–40, *see also*
  ideal family
competitiveness,
  with biological parent, 80–4, 149–50,
  159–60
complications of step-family life, 71–92
  and money, 72–8
confidence, *see* self-confidence
conflict, 46

206 INDEX

custodial parent, *see* biological parent
custody, 191–3, *see also* access

denying problems, *see* problems
differences between biological and
    step-families, 27–33
  children's perceptions, 83–4
divided loyalties, *see* loyalty
discipline, 93–117
  defining, 93
  and fear, 96
  problems of, 93–9
  purposes of, 97–101
  see also anger, punishment, rewards

emotional hypochondria, 25
emotions, mixed, *see* mixed emotions
example, step-parent as, 69
excuses, *see* understanding

favouritism, 129–33
  biological over step-children, 130–2
  handling, 132–3
  and 'ideal family', 129–31
  when legitimate, 131
fetchers and carriers, adults as, 10,
    61–3
  and care, 62
  and communication, 63
  and love, 62
  see also role of step-parent
folklore, *see* fiction, myths
fiction, 203
functionaries, adults as, *see* fetchers and
    carriers

gender of step-parent, 11
'good behaviour', 96, 101–2, 104
  not always desirable, 96, 101–2
  see also 'bad behaviour'
grandparents, 89–92
  favouritism and, 92
  importance of, 90–1
  and loss, 163–4
  maintaining contact with, 90–1
  respecting feelings of, 89–92
  step-grandparents, 91–2
Grimm, Brothers, *see* myths
guilt, 26, 34–9
  and access, 81
  causes of, 35–7
  and discipline, 98–9
  effects of, 36–7

handling, 37–9, 178–9
and money, 73

healing aspects of step-families, 33–4
help, 24, 76
  sources of, 197–200
high standards, 37–9, 61
history of step-families, 44
homosexual step-families, 11

ideal family, 39–40, 129–31
image of step-families, 9, 14–15, 25,
    41–5, *see also* myths
inexperience, *see* 'bad behaviour'
ingratiation, *see* 'good behaviour',
    rewards
inheritance, *see* history, wills
innocence, children's, 165–6
instant families, 128–9, 168, 185–6

jealousy, 124–9
  and affection, 125–6
  dealing with, 127–9
  defining, 124–5
  as envy, 124–5
  and instant families, 128–9
  as possessiveness, 124–5
  recognising, 124, 126–7
  and time, 125–6

kinship, 27, 44
knowledge, as need of children, 69–71
  nature of, 69

law, 191–6, 203–4
literature, 41–2, *see also* fiction, myths
loss, 142–66
  and biological parent, 175–6
  and child's age, 150–4
  of childhood innocence, 165–6
  circumstances, 145–6
  consolations, 162–3
  denial of, 146–7
  factors affecting impact, 145–65
  and grandparents, 163–4
  handling, 154–60
  idealising the lost person, 147–9,
    159–60
  and magical thinking, 152–4
  and money, 161–2
  and step-children, 142–66
  varieties, 145–6

love, 20–21, 33–4, 45–8, 58–61, 121–2,
    126–8
    as a child's need, 58–61
    and care, 59–63
    nature of, 58–61
    and tenderness, 58–9
    and warmth, 59
    where available, 60–61
    see also care
loyalty, 28
    divided, 82–3, 176–8

maintenance payments, 32, 73–4
mixed emotions, 14–15, 45–8
    and names, 87
money, 72–8
    emotional significance of, 73–5, 78
    and family breakup, 161–2
    insurance payouts, 75
    sorting out problems, 77–8
    and wills, 75–6
moral basis of step-families, 28–9
morality, teaching of, 32, 101–2
myths, 41–5, 202

names, 84–9
    and absent parent, 88
    and care, 88–9
    choice of surname, 85–6, 185
    emotional significance of, 84–6
    forms of address, 86–8
    legal aspects of, 194–5
    and misunderstanding, 85
naughtiness, see 'bad behaviour'
needs, 57–71
    adults', 48
    children's, 57–71
    meaning of, 55–7
    and wishes, 56–7
    see also care, fetchers and carriers,
        knowledge, love, security, sense of
        worth, stimulation

over-protectiveness, 98–9

parent
    absent, see absent parent
    biological, see biological parent
    custodial, see biological parent
parenthood, learning, 53
passports, 196
pensions, 75, see also money
perfectionism, see high standards

power, and punishment, 112–3
practical child-care, 10
    and love, 59
protection
    and discipline, 98–9
    see also over-protectiveness
pride
    in being a step-parent, 30, 37–8
    in parenthood, 116, 130–131
privacy, 125
problems, denial of, 24
punishment, 106–116
    avoiding, 117
    formal, 108–112
    inadvisability of, 106–8
    informal, 109
    justification, 107–8
    and power, 112–3
    and relationships, 116–7
    see also rewards, security

quarrels, 39–40, 46–8, 187

realism, 59
reputation of step-parents, see myths
research, 43–4, 118, 201
resentment, 61, 73
    and money, 73–6
rewards
    and discipline, 113–6
    formal, 114–5
    informal, 114–5
    and ingratiation, 113–4
    and relationships, 116–7
    of step-parenting, 15–16
role of step-parent
    as brother or sister, 32–3
    as friend, 31–2
    as role model, 69
    as servant, 10, 61–3
    source of care, 20–1, 59–60, 62–3
    source of love, 58–60
    source of security, 64–8
    as surrogate parent, 31
    as teacher, 69–71
routine
    and care, 59–60
    and jealousy, 128
    and sex, 121
    and stress on biological parent, 180–1
rules, see security
'rules of the game', see knowledge

208 INDEX

scapegoating, 134–8
  damage done by, 134–8
  dealing with, 136–8
  recognising, 135
  and self-fulfilling prophesies, 135
  uses of, 136–7
security, 64–8
self-confidence, 26
self-forgiveness, *see* guilt
self-knowledge, 80–1, 99–100, 109–11
  and access, 83–4
  and biological parent, 178–9
  and favouritism, 132
  and jealousy, 126–7
  and money, 76–8
  and sex, 119–23
sense of worth, 57–8, 99–101
sex, 118–23
  and affection, 122
  avoiding danger, 119–23
  damaging effects of, 119
  seductive behaviour, 122–4
  step-brother and step-sister, 123
  step-father and daughter, 118–23
social security, 72–3, 198, *see also* money
step-children,
  in autobiography, 203
  in fiction, 203
  needs, 57–71
  understanding, 141–66
step-families,
  different from biological families, 29, 30, 37, 39–40, 70
  history of, 44
  hopes and fears, 167–71
  images of, 168–71
  pitfalls of, 118–38, 182–7
step-parents,
  as carers, *see* care, role of step-parent

competitiveness with biological
  parent, 63, 80–4, 149–50, 159–60
and disappointment, 169–70
excluding children, 183–4
legal rights and responsibilities, 195
misuse of children, 182–7
as outsiders, 185–6
rescue fantasies, 170–1
as role model, *see* role of step-parents
as surrogate parents, *see* role of step-parents
as teachers, *see* role of step-parent
wicked, *see* image, myths, research
step-grandparents, *see* grandparents
stimulation, 57

talking about problems, 179–80
  not always appropriate, 77, 121–2
  and step-children
teaching, *see* role of step-parent
testing behaviour, 68
time, *see* jealousy, loss
  and healing, 187
tolerance, 23

understanding, 142–187
  adults, 167–87
  benefits, 22
  dangers of, 22–3
  and excuses, 22–3
  importance, 21–7
  step-children, 142–166
unhappiness, *see* 'bad behaviour'

weekend step-children, 10
wicked step-parents, *see* myths
wills, 75–6
  and the law, 195